D0898037

ROMANOFF AND JULIET

ROMANOFF

AND

JULIET

A COMEDY IN THREE ACTS

by Peter Ustinov

RANDOM HOUSE · NEW YORK

Romanoff and Juliet *was first presented by David Merrick at the Plymouth Theatre, New York City, on October 10, 1957, with the following cast:*

(IN ORDER OF APPEARANCE)

First Soldier	Phil Leeds
Second Soldier	Jack Gilford
The General	Peter Ustinov
Hooper Moulsworth	Fred Clark
Vadim Romanoff	Henry Lascoe
Igor Romanoff	Gerald Sarracini
Juliet Moulsworth	Elizabeth Allen
The Spy	Carl Don
Beulah Moulsworth	Natalie Schafer
Evdokia Romanoff	Marianne Deeming
Jr. Captain Marfa Zlotochienko	Sylvia Daneel
Freddie Vandestuyt	William Greene
The Archbishop	Edward Atienza

Staged by George S. Kaufman

Setting by Denis Malcles

Settings and Lighting supervised by Howard Bay

Costumes by Helene Pons

Incidental Music by Harold Rome

Ballads by Anthony Hopkins *and* Peter Ustinov

The main square in the capital city of the smallest country in Europe

ACT ONE

Dawn to morning

ACT TWO

Noon to afternoon

ACT THREE

Evening to night

ACT ONE

Act One

Dawn to morning.

The main square in the capital city of the smallest country in Europe. It is dawn. A somber building on the left, with a balcony. In the background, a cathedral with an illuminated clock, on which a great many unsteady saints frequently appear together with Father Time, Death the Reaper and other allegorical figures, to hammer out fractions of the hour. A somber building on the right, with a balcony. The sky is expansive, and has the crystalline purity of early dawn in the south.

Two soldiers lie in the shadows, one near each house. They are on guard.

FIRST SOLDIER Your turn to start.

SECOND SOLDIER T.

FIRST SOLDIER R.

SECOND SOLDIER T.R . . . A.

FIRST SOLDIER N.

SECOND SOLDIER T.R.A.N . . . S.

FIRST SOLDIER U.

SECOND SOLDIER U? No such word.

FIRST SOLDIER Yes, there is.

SECOND SOLDIER Well, if there is, it's not spelled that way.

FIRST SOLDIER Yes, it is.

SECOND SOLDIER Ah!

FIRST SOLDIER Ah!. . .

SECOND SOLDIER T.R.A.N.S.U.B.

FIRST SOLDIER S.

SECOND SOLDIER T.

FIRST SOLDIER A.

SECOND SOLDIER N.

FIRST SOLDIER T.

SECOND SOLDIER I.

FIRST SOLDIER A.

SECOND SOLDIER T.

FIRST SOLDIER I. Oh, damn.

SECOND SOLDIER You should have forseen that O.(*Long pause*) I said O.

FIRST SOLDIER I still don't think it's spelled that way.

SECOND SOLDIER Go on. Say it. N.

FIRST SOLDIER Transubstantiation? I am sure that it's got three S's somewhere.

SECOND SOLDIER I gave you rhododendron just now, although I'm damn sure there're two H's in it.

FIRST SOLDIER All right, all right. What's that make it?

SECOND SOLDIER (*Consulting a bit of paper awkwardly in the dark*) Eight twenty-four to seven sixty-seven.

FIRST SOLDIER Who's eight twenty-four?

SECOND SOLDIER I am.
(*He puts the paper and pencil in his pocket*)

FIRST SOLDIER I won't argue. It only goes to show that the night's too long.

SECOND SOLDIER It's nearly over. (*He consults his watch*) Death is late.

FIRST SOLDIER They don't know how to oil him properly.

SECOND SOLDIER Your turn to start . . . (*Looks offstage and rises rapidly, coming to stiff attention*) Look out! A General. (*A figure appears in the uniform of an operetta general, sky blue and silver.* FIRST SOLDIER *rises and stands at attention*)

GENERAL Good morning.

FIRST SOLDIER

SECOND SOLDIER
} Good morning.

GENERAL Aren't you rather forgetting something?
(FIRST *and* SECOND SOLDIERS *look blank for a moment, then hurriedly pick up their guns*)

SECOND SOLDIER (*Colloquial*) Regiment pre-sent—are you ready?

FIRST SOLDIER Yes, only hurry, it's heavy.

SECOND SOLDIER Pre-sent—ahms!
(*They do so, with insulting untidiness*)

GENERAL (*Saluting, with a sigh*) Thank you very much.

FIRST SOLDIER Don't mention it.

GENERAL (*Takes out a heavy gold watch*) Any sign of Death yet?

SECOND SOLDIER No, sir.

GENERAL I make him ten minutes late.
(*There's a strange sound of creaking machinery. They all look at the clock. The wobbling figure of Death the Reaper emerges and hits a bell with sickening force. The sound produced, however, is dull and unresonant*)

FIRST SOLDIER He's getting old.

GENERAL Fourteenth century. Hardly adolescent by our standards.

FIRST SOLDIER (*Bitterly*) Our standards.

GENERAL You must be a Socialist, young man.

FIRST SOLDIER Socialist Agrarian Reform Peasants' Industrial Party. (*Salutes strangely*)

GENERAL I've never heard of it.

FIRST SOLDIER I'm a founder member.

SECOND SOLDIER I don't hold with his views, General.

GENERAL Oh, perhaps you belong to my party?

SECOND SOLDIER National Iron Fist. The Nif. (*He salutes strangely*) We wear violet shirts . . . or would if we could afford them.

6

GENERAL No, I'm Rally of Unionist Separatist Extremes, sometimes known as the R.U.S.E. Anyone—?

FIRST SOLDIER No.

SECOND SOLDIER Sorry . . .

GENERAL How strange. It's the party at present in power. In fact I am President of the Republic.

SECOND SOLDIER At the moment?

GENERAL Yes. I have been for some ten hours.

FIRST SOLDIER You're doing well.
    (*Extends his right hand*)

GENERAL Well I—Oh, may I? (*Shakes* FIRST SOLDIER's *hand*) Thank you very much. (*With a sigh*) Yes. We judge a dog's life as being roughly one-seventh that of a man. But a president doesn't deserve even a dog's life. (*Laughs. He suddenly looks out front and is surprised to see the audience. He is immediately on his most courtly behavior*) Oh,—Look at us— (*Both soldiers challenge the audience as they see it for the first time*)

FIRST SOLDIER Halt!

SECOND SOLDIER Who goes there?

GENERAL Put your rifles away.

SECOND SOLDIER It may be wiser. We're outnumbered.

FIRST SOLDIER Are those people out there in the shadows?

GENERAL Yes, and we must be polite to them; we're entirely dependent on our tourist trade. (*He addresses the audience*) Good evening. You will find us only on the very best atlases, because we are the smallest country left in Europe—and when I say country I don't mean principality or grand duchy. I don't mean a haven for gambling and income tax evasion—No, I mean a self-respecting country which deserves, and sometimes achieves a color of its own on the map. This is usually a particularly dyspeptic mint green which misses the outline of the frontier by a fraction of an inch, so that one can almost hear the printer saying damn. In fourteen seventy-one we attracted the attention of the world by failing to stop the Turks—in a bloodless battle not two streets away from here—in the suburbs. And there are many other people we have failed to stop on other occasions, so you can see that our country is steeped in history, and makes for a fascinating and a different holiday, which we hope you will enjoy. Our population is so small that it's hardly worth counting. We have no cannons, we need no fodder. (SECOND SOLDIER *clicks his rifle, and in adjusting strap, points gun at the* GENERAL) Don't fiddle with your rifle—there's a sport. It's dangerous.

SECOND SOLDIER They're only blanks.

GENERAL (*Shocked*) I should hope so!

SECOND SOLDIER Do you mean that, as a General, you're not the tiniest bit ambitious for our military future?

GENERAL I prefer our military past. The harm's done, and there it is. As for being a General, well, at the age of four, with paper hats and wooden swords, we're *all* Generals. Some of us never grow out of it.
(*He sits on bench, left*)

SECOND SOLDIER But—aren't you proud of the fact that we won the last war?

FIRST SOLDIER No one won the last war.

8

GENERAL   We tactfully declared war on Germany several hours before her surrender. As a consequence we were offered six acres of land which didn't belong to us, by the grateful Allies. This we cleverly refused. The result is that we are now on good terms with everyone.

FIRST SOLDIER   You live in the past, General. Our future lies in the abolition of frontiers. The day will dawn when the workers will tear down the customs sheds and extend the hand of friendship across the artificial gulfs imposed by nationalists and capitalist warmongers.

GENERAL   (*Pause—sadly*)   You read a great deal, don't you?

SECOND SOLDIER   To my mind, every mother who has successfully borne five children should be given a free issue of toy bayonets by a grateful nation.

GENERAL   And yet, my dear friends, our love for what is ours is far subtler, far deeper than all your silly foreign ideas. And I'll prove it to you. I only have to start singing a folk song for you two to join in—despite your better judgment.

FIRST SOLDIER

SECOND SOLDIER
}   (*Derisively*) Folk song!

GENERAL   Folk song! (*Singing softly, and with love*)

> An angel weary of Paradise
> Came down to visit the Earth.
> She floated over hill and dale
> Till she heard laughter and mirth.
>
> What is that ripple of happiness
> That wafts through the trees like a song

What is that shout of banners
Which crowns the distant throng?

It's our army of rocking horses
Off to a bloodless war.
It's our princes and our captains
On their way to the sandy shore.

Our swords are made of good white wood.
Our castles are built of sand.
Our lances are made of plasticine;
We're off to defend our land!
Our land! Our land!
We're off to defend our land!

The angel returned to Paradise
A younger, wiser girl.
She swore she'd never journey again.
Her head was in a whirl.
For as the sky has its Paradise
So the Earth has its pearl;
Our country! Our country!
The Earth has its pearl!

(*Gradually the other two have joined in, at first hum-
ming the melody, then singing elaborately and fluently
in parts. They finish. The upstairs French doors of the
building on the audience's right open with a clatter. An
angry man in pajamas looks out. A mask hangs around
his neck*)

ANGRY MAN Hey! Can't a guy get a decent night's rest around
here? If it isn't the cathedral clock, it's drunks!

GENERAL Drunks? I beg your pardon, Mr. Ambassador!

ANGRY MAN (*Rubbing the sleep out of his eyes*) Who's that?
Oh, Mr. President—please forgive my outburst. It was a great
party last night. Or should I say this morning?

GENERAL Thank you.

ANGRY MAN The idea of wearing masks was just great.

GENERAL (*Modest*) It's traditional.

ANGRY MAN Hey! I still have mine on! What do you know?
The damndest thing! Well, sure makes me wish you had
Independence Day every day.

GENERAL We do, but we can't afford to celebrate it more than
ten or fifteen times a year.

ANGRY MAN Is that so?

GENERAL We have won our independence at least four hundred times, which makes us cumulatively the most independ-
ent people in Europe.

ANGRY MAN Is that so? Well, that's certainly worth knowing.

WOMAN (*Voice*) Hooper!

ANGRY MAN Coming, sugar.

WOMAN (*Voice*) Are you crazy, standing in that window with
your arthritis?

ANGRY MAN (*Sheepish*) Well, I guess you fellows heard. See
you. (*He goes*)

FIRST SOLDIER (*Sour*) Warmonger!
(*The reciprocating window in the house opposite opens
and another angry man looks out*)

SECOND ANGRY MAN   Psst!

GENERAL   Ambassador! Good morning.

SECOND ANGRY MAN   He said something?

GENERAL   Who?

SECOND ANGRY MAN   I can hear him speak if I put my ear to the window, but I can only catch the sounds, not the words.

GENERAL   We woke him with our singing. I hope we didn't do the same to you.

SECOND ANGRY MAN   I don't sleep.

GENERAL   Never?

SECOND ANGRY MAN   Never.

GENERAL   Insomnia?

SECOND ANGRY MAN   Policy.

GENERAL   Gracious.

SECOND ANGRY MAN   May I congratulate you, Mr. President, on the reception last night, which perceptibly increased our solidarity?

GENERAL   I enjoyed it. I was the last to leave, and got rather drunk.

SECOND ANGRY MAN (*Without humor*)   Drunkenness in pursuit of solidarity is not a sin.

WOMAN (*Voice, strident*)   Vadim!

SECOND ANGRY MAN   Da, golubka.

WOMAN (*Voice*)   Paidi Suda!

12

SECOND ANGRY MAN (*Conciliatory*) Sichas, sichas . . .

GENERAL You'd better go.

SECOND ANGRY MAN (*Suspicious*) You understand our language?

GENERAL No—I understand . . . the situation.
> (*Abruptly the* SECOND ANGRY MAN *disappears. A decrepit saint strikes the bell*)

GENERAL St. Simon Stylites. . . . I make it seven sixteen.

FIRST SOLDIER (*Consulting watch*) Seven o four.

SECOND SOLDIER (*Consulting watch*) A quarter to eight.

FIRST SOLDIER That clock's a national disgrace.

SECOND SOLDIER For once I agree with you.

GENERAL Why? The only one who's always punctual is Death . . . . Whatever the time, he always strikes his knell at the first streak of dawn . . . and believe me, he knows what he's doing. How I hate the dawn! It's the hour of the firing squad. The last glass of brandy. The final wish. The ultimate cigarette. All the hideously calculated hypocrisy of men when they commit a murder in the name of justice. Then it's the time of Death on a grander scale, the hour of the great offensives . . . fix your bayonets, boys . . . Gentlemen, synchronize your watches . . . in ten seconds' time the barrage begins . . . a thousand men are destined to die in order to capture a farmhouse no one has lived in for years. . . . And finally, dawn is the herald of the day, our twelve hours of unimportance, when we have to cede to the pressure of the powers, smile at people we have every reason but expediency to detest. . . . A diplomat these days is nothing but a headwaiter who's allowed to sit down occasionally . . . (*Playing to the house on audience's left*) . . . and how do you want your imports . . . in oil? In gasoline! Well done? Rare! Your taste is impeccable, if I may say so, sir. May I say so, sir? Thank you very much. (*Playing to the house on audience's right*) Yes, sir? Of course, I guarantee not to serve the other diner with any secrets . . . I'll tell him that secrets are off the menu—although you and I know, don't we, sir—? Ha, ha, ha—(*Surprised*) Sir, service is included. . . . Oh, well . . . if you insist . . . (*With elaborate gratitude, bowing deeply*) Thank *you very* much. . . . (*He comes up from his deep bow and looks searchingly at the soldiers*) You hate the night because you find it boring. . . . I hate the day because it's an insult to my intelligence, a slur on my honor, a worm in the heart of my integrity, whereas the night . . . (*He basks in his thought*) The night is marvelous . . . because it is the time when the great powers are asleep, conserving their energies for the horrors of the ensuing day . . . and in that time of magic and of mystery our horizons are infinite . . . they stretch not only to the north and to the south, the east and west, but up towards the moon, down towards the center of the earth. In peace, and in harmony with nature, we send out our vast battalions to colonize—the imagination. . . . While others sleep, our Empire knows no bounds. (*A cock crows. The street lamps go out. He sits heavily*) There. Our daily winter has begun.

SECOND SOLDIER (*Softly*) Look.

GENERAL Oh, look. (*He rises, picking up his hat, and crosses to stand between the soldiers. He holds the hat in front of his face and peeks through the plumes.* FIRST *and* SECOND SOLDIERS *move back a step. A pair of lovers have wandered into the square, too involved in each other to know where they are. They wear evening dress, and a mask dangles from a ribbon around her neck. They kiss passionately. The* GENERAL *continues softly. Heartfelt*) Oh, I hope they found each other very early in the night, for now he may notice a wrinkle under the weary, longing eye, while she may spy a trace of cruel satisfaction around his mouth. Let us be tactful.

(*He puts on his hat*)

FIRST SOLDIER (*Loud*)   My turn to give the order.

GENERAL   Sh! Tactful!

FIRST SOLDIER (*Whispering*)   Regiment. Salute the flag! Dismiss!

(*They all salute in their chaotic way, and then tiptoe out with a last sentimental look at the lovers. The lovers break from a long, long kiss and look at each other in adoration*)

HE   Are there words which have not been used before?

SHE   There are silences which have not been shared before. Why do you look at me so critically?

HE   Critically?

SHE   Are there bags under my eyes?

HE   I would be lying if I told you you weren't tired.

SHE (*Hiding her face*)   Then don't look at me.

HE (*Turning her face to him again*)   I want to guess what you will look like at seventy.

SHE   It's late. We're getting silly. It's the sunlight and the weariness and the sad farewell of old champagne on the

15

tongue. There was no edge to our thoughts when the candles and the cut-glass ornaments sent shivering milky ways up to the ceiling, and when your eyes sparkled like mineral wealth from the rock of your face.

HE (*Sadly*)   You can't recapture it by language.

SHE   I know.

HE   Enchantment fades so quickly, that after five minutes you doubt if it was ever there.

SHE (*Desperately*)   But I am still here!

HE (*Clasping her*)   Yes, a warm, a living thing, which I desire. Last night we were as one, creatures in a dream, selflessly united in an endless waltz. From now on we are opposed, a man and a woman in love . . . the greatest, the most exhausting struggle in the world. Two moths racing for the flame—two cannibals devouring each other.

SHE   Have you known many women?

HE   I am a sailor by profession.

SHE   Thank you for your honesty.

HE   You have never kissed a man?

SHE   Only four. And Freddie.

HE   What do you mean—only four, and Freddie? Do you mean five?

SHE   Five? (*Surprised, she turns it over in her mind*) No, I mean four—and Freddie.

HE   Who's Freddie?

SHE (*Enraptured*)   You're jealous!

HE   I'm waiting for an answer.

SHE   Freddie? He's my fiancé.

HE   I see.

SHE   (*A little foolishly*)   He's in refrigerators.

HE   I don't understand.

SHE   He makes refrigerators. His father made refrigerators before him.

HE   A hereditary gift.

SHE   Freddie believes he has a mission in refrigeration. He told me once when he was drunk that in the event of war he has a device which can freeze the Gulf Stream and make everyone but us very uncomfortable. Oh, Lord, I shouldn't be telling you this, should I?

HE   No.

SHE   You have no accent, darling. I keep forgetting who you are.

HE   (*With pomp*)   I serve aboard the icebreaker *Red October*. Ironic, isn't it, that it may one day be my duty to crash through Freddie's most cherished daydream.

SHE   Oh, how awful. Now everything's spoiled.

HE   (*Kindly*)   Why? Surely love recognizes no didactic frontiers?

SHE   No, it doesn't, but what a ghastly way of saying so.

HE   Ghastly? What is so ghastly about a clear thought, clearly expressed?

17

SHE (*Intensely*) But, Igor! "Creatures in a dream, selflessly united in an endless waltz—"

HE I said that, didn't I?

SHE Yes.

HE Curious how romance tricks the otherwise logical mind into inaccuracies. Naturally, the waltz could not have been endless, otherwise it would still be going on—(*He notices her incredulous face*)—and that is impossible, since we are now here.

SHE (*In real agony*) Oh, no!

HE (*Suddenly*) Does what I say sound very humorless and . . . and un-Western when I talk like that? (*Silence*) I must apologize. I can never regret a phenomenon as beautiful or as powerful as our love, but I must admit that it has created within me the most reprehensible ideological confusion. I must consult my textbooks before I can hope to interpret to you in scientific terms the exact extent of my spiritual deviation.

SHE (*Hopeful*) You mean you love me more than Marx?

HE (*Sharply*) Please do not speak sarcastically. It doesn't suit you.

SHE I'm sorry, but I'm jealous of the man.

HE I do not make light of your beliefs.

SHE (*Tenderly*) I can't make you out.

HE (*Depressed*) I can't make myself out. It's all so simple in the Arctic.

SHE Do you blame the climate, my darling?

HE No. No, it's relatively simple in the Black Sea also.

SHE Women? Women in general. Do they confuse you, dearest?

HE Women? I've known women before. I served on a ship under a woman captain, although in fairness to her, you wouldn't have guessed that she was a woman. *She* did not disturb me in the least. (*Slowly, and with considerable difficulty*) The fact is—I love you.

SHE (*Ecstatic*) Oh . . .

HE (*Severe*) Please don't interrupt me. For my own good, for our future, I must analyze my reasons for loving you in spite of vast and irreconcilable spiritual and political divergencies. First of all, we were wearing masks. Your mask could have hidden the eager face of a freckled collective-farm girl.

SHE Oh, Igor, that's not true. No collective-farm girl has an American accent.

HE Yes, I was cheating. Forgive me. (*Fierce*) I must be honest with myself. I think I know what drew me irresistibly towards you.

SHE (*Coquettish*) What is it?

HE (*Very serious*) You couldn't possibly be the captain of a ship. You're one of the only women I've ever met who couldn't possibly be the captain of a ship.

SHE Dad bought me a dinghy last fall. It's moored near Cape Cod. I love the sea, angel, just the way you do.

HE (*Gently*) Could you bring a six-thousand-ton cargo ship into Murmansk harbor . . . without a pilot . . . backwards . . . in a snowstorm?

SHE I've never tried.

HE No, you couldn't. And nor could I. Glory to our women trawler captains.

SHE Glory to them indeed. Kiss me.

HE Not yet. I must first reach certain ethical conclusions.

SHE Igor, there's so little time! Kiss me!

HE I forbid—

SHE You want to.

HE No.

SHE Please!

HE Thank you.

> (*They embrace and lose themselves in the silent game of love, oblivious to all around them. The two soldiers reappear, one from either side, now dressed as peasants in rags. Both carry merchandise aimed at the tourist market*)

FIRST SOLDIER Peanuts, traditional salted marzipan, raffia table-runners, English collar studs, back numbers of *True Detective* magazine.

SECOND SOLDIER Keepsakes, bangles, prehistoric coins; religious postcards, beautifully picked out in silk and sequins.

} *Together*

SECOND SOLDIER There's nothing more suitable to announce your engagement than a nice religious postcard.

FIRST SOLDIER No table is complete without raffia table-runners, and, incidentally, I can supply the table as well.

SECOND SOLDIER Cupid's indiscretions, smuggled into the country only last Wednesday—

SHE (*Angry*) Oh, please leave us alone!
  (*Resumes kiss*)

SECOND SOLDIER This is a free country, madam. We have a right to share your privacy in a public place.
  (*The* GENERAL *enters, now dressed in a morning suit*)

GENERAL What? Still at it? This must be what they call the real thing.

SECOND SOLDIER It must be. It's death to commerce.

GENERAL The real thing! And I don't even know the false thing.

SHE (*Spinning around, furious*) Oh, please—!

GENERAL (*Amazed; adjusting his pince-nez and saluting*) Miss Moulsworth!

SHE Sh! Don't tell Dad, please!

GENERAL I envied your idyl without ever realizing that it involved the much-admired Miss Juliet. Merciful heavens, Lieutenant Romanoff!

HE Silence! (*He looks around nervously*) I implore you not to say a word of this to anyone. If you do, my career is finished. (GENERAL *laughs*) Why do you laugh?

GENERAL I began my life as a ne'er-do-well, but was discovered cheating at cards. My career was finished. Look at me now.
  (*He indicates the medals on his coat*)

HE You are confusing me!

SHE   Oh, please don't confuse him.

GENERAL   But are you really in love? I ask as an innocent, not as a technician.

SHE   Yes, only he won't let himself go. It's psychological. He's got to the stage of sorting out his emotions, and kind of freeing them from all those men, you know, Marx, Lenin, Trotsky.

HE (*Violent*)   Trotsky! I can never forgive you for that!

GENERAL (*Hastily*)   She meant Engels. The names are somewhat similar. You need my help.

HE
}   No.
SHE

GENERAL   Yes, I can see from your utter misery, from your eagerness to misunderstand each other, and from your thoroughly bad temper, that this is the real thing. You wish to meet again tonight?

HE
}   No.
SHE

GENERAL   Very well, I'll see what I can do. Tonight is the thousandth anniversary of our liberation from the—Lithuanians.

FIRST SOLDIER   Is it really? I thought—

GENERAL   Yes! It may not have been a thousand years ago, and it almost certainly wasn't the Lithuanians, but we celebrate whatever it was tonight, and that's an order.

SECOND SOLDIER   With fireworks?

GENERAL With whatever we can afford.

(SECOND SOLDIER *draws two very small rockets from his tray, and offers them for inspection to the* GENERAL)

GENERAL (*Approvingly*) Two fireworks. Well done! It will be dark at eight o'clock. (*He looks at the couple, who are kissing again*) Does eight o'clock seem very long to wait? I know. Try to be patient.

HE (*Abruptly*) Good-bye.

GENERAL That's right. This is no time for emotion. Bear your separation with fortitude.

SHE I'm going.

GENERAL That's it. Bite your lip, like a heroine. (*The lovers are tempted to look back as they reach the doors of their respective embassies*) No, resist temptation! Orpheus, don't look back at Eurydice! There are only twelve hours of Hades. Earn your joy tonight! (*Precipitately, the lovers disappear. The* GENERAL *sighs romantically. The soldiers dry their eyes*) We're a sentimental people.

FIRST SOLDIER I'm glad I didn't sell any of those stinking table-runners . . . they deserve better . . .

SECOND SOLDIER And my postcards are in such bad taste . . .

GENERAL Oh, my God! (*With sudden anguish*) I thought of it as a love story, beautiful, pure, simple. Simple? . . . It's a diplomatic earthquake!

(*As the* GENERAL *goes to one side to brood about this disturbing realization, a man enters dressed as a spy, looking too anonymous to be possible. He goes quickly and silently to the* SECOND SOLDIER)

SPY Have they arrived?

SECOND SOLDIER Eh?

SPY What I ordered.

SECOND SOLDIER Oh, it's you . . . yes . . .
(*He produces a small packet or two surreptitiously*)

SPY Is this all?

SECOND SOLDIER For the moment.

SPY How much?

SECOND SOLDIER Eight hundred.

SPY Too much.

SECOND SOLDIER They cost me almost that.

SPY (*Putting them in his pocket*) Put them on my account.

SECOND SOLDIER But when?—

SPY You will be paid. And remember—you have seen nothing.
I never talked to you. I don't exist.
(*The* SPY *vanishes into the Russian Embassy*)

FIRST SOLDIER What's all that about? Since when have you had
commercial relations with the Russians?

SECOND SOLDIER Even a Fascist must live. I supply him with
postcards.

FIRST SOLDIER Who is he?

SECOND SOLDIER Isn't it obvious?

GENERAL (*Suddenly*) Men, I need your help.

24

FIRST SOLDIER We're off duty.

GENERAL We are all in the service of the god of Love.

SECOND SOLDIER But we can't live on our military pay alone.

GENERAL (*Angry*) What is the meaning of this mercenary prattle? Just now you shed a tear for them. Is it in the traditions of our country to confuse love with high finance?

SECOND SOLDIER No, it isn't. That's what's wrong with us.

GENERAL (*Unexpectedly military*) What did you say? Regiment! About—wait for the order! About—face! In step this time. This is war. Left-right-left.

(These orders should be as loud and as incomprehensible as those of any army, and the bafflement of the soldiers in the face of this inhuman caterwauling should awaken uncomfortable memories in all male hearts. The interior of the American Embassy revolves onto the stage, decorated in the pompous official style, with JULIET's very feminine bedroom above it. JULIET sits in the drawing room in an attitude of deep dejection. The door opens, and MR. AMBASSADOR MOULSWORTH enters)

MOULSWORTH Well, and how's my girl? Tired, heh? Don't I get my kiss? Hey, I got news to put the sparkle back in your eye.

JULIET (*Fiercely*) Dad, I've got to tell you something.

MOULSWORTH (*Good-humored*) O.K., and I won't tell Freddie.

JULIET (*Amazed*) You know, then?

MOULSWORTH Sure, I saw you . . . and let me tell you something, the guy you were with . . . well, he was a tribute to your taste, and there's no reason on God's green earth why Freddie should ever know . . .

JULIET (*Pale*)   You liked Igor?

MOULSWORTH   Who's that?

JULIET   The boy I was with.

MOULSWORTH   Yeah. Swell physique. Great golfer, I bet. What was his name again?

JULIET   Igor.

MOULSWORTH   Well, what's in a name? I once had a classmate called Epiphany. Anyway, that's all over now. (*He beams*) Now, listen to this, baby. Are you ready?

JULIET (*Emotional*)   Dad, if you've got good news, give it to me. I need it.
   (BEULAH MOULSWORTH *enters*)

BEULAH   And how's my daughter this morning?
   (*She kisses* JULIET)

JULIET   Hi, Mom!

BEULAH   Have you told her, Hooper?

MOULSWORTH (*Touchy*)   I'm on the point of doing so, Beulah. (*Beaming*) Great news, Julie—

BEULAH   Great news indeed. You're a big girl now—

MOULSWORTH (*With terrible patience*)   Let me handle this, Beulah. Julie—

JULIET   Yes?

MOULSWORTH Freddie!

JULIET What about him?

MOULSWORTH He's flying in on the midday clipper!

JULIET (*Pale*) Oh, no . . .
(*She sways forward*)

MOULSWORTH What's the matter with her?

BEULAH Get some water, Hooper. She's fainted . . . There, there, Mother's here, Mother's here. (BEULAH *cradles* JULIET *in her arms. Sarcastic*) You'll handle it, Beulah. You're just the most tactful man I've ever met, that's all.

MOULSWORTH (*Who has poured a glass of water*) I'm forthright.

BEULAH Juliet's a girl, Hooper. A girl. Girls don't like forthrightness.

MOULSWORTH Well, what do you expect me to say?—"A little bird told me that you-know-who is flying in today?"

BEULAH Girls thrive on a lingering uncertainty . . . on a tremulous half-doubt . . . I know. I was a girl myself.

MOULSWORTH First things first. How is she?

BEULAH Coming 'round, oh, so slowly. She's sensitive.

MOULSWORTH We're all sensitive. (*Beaming*) How's my honey?

JULIET (*Softly*) Dad . . .

MOULSWORTH Yeah, here I am, right here.

JULIET I've got to tell you . . . I am not in love with Freddie.

MOULSWORTH Not in—? Now, wait a minute.

BEULAH She must have calm, Hooper.

MOULSWORTH So must I have calm.

BEULAH Up to bed, my only sweet one.

JULIET (*Rising*) I'm going . . . but first I've got to tell you . . . I'm in love with Igor.

BEULAH (*A girl again*) There's someone else. . . . What's he like?

JULIET Dad saw him.

MOULSWORTH Beulah, this is far too serious to accept as a matter of course. Remember, Freddie's flying out here at his own expense. Who is this other guy?

JULIET Igor Vadimovitch Romanoff, the son of their Ambassador.

MOULSWORTH (*A great shout*) What!

JULIET (*Quiet*) I'll go lie down now.
  (*She goes out. Long pause*)

BEULAH Maybe we didn't treat her right when she was a baby . . .

MOULSWORTH (*With suppressed majesty*) Beulah, there comes a time in the life of every parent when—

BEULAH (*Suddenly violent*) Oh, Hooper, this isn't a board meeting!

MOULSWORTH (*Shouting back*) She must know what she's doing to me . . . her father! Why, if this ever gets out! Board meeting! You can sit there and tell me—

BEULAH I never was sold on Freddie being right for her. (JULIET *enters the bedroom upstairs and sprawls across the bed*)

MOULSWORTH That is neither here nor there. Freddie's father rowed in my boat at Princeton, but I am deliberately forgetting all that—all my personal loyalties. The fact is that our only daughter has fallen for a Commie—a Communist, Beulah—and when I say Communist, Beulah, I don't just mean a guy who sent a food package to the wrong side of Spain, Beulah—I mean the son of a high-ranking Soviet executive!

BEULAH Why must you always show everything up in its worst possible light!

MOULSWORTH Don't talk so loud, Beulah . . . the walls in this city are not exactly soundproof.

BEULAH Why did we have to come to this God-forsaken country in the first place? Our Embassy practically next door to the Reds . . . we're just asking for trouble.

MOULSWORTH I knew you'd say something along those lines. It's like when I catch a cold . . . your first reaction is not how will I get rid of it, but where did I catch it.

BEULAH Don't tell me you've got a cold?

MOULSWORTH No, I do not have a cold!

BEULAH I wonder where you caught it.

MOULSWORTH I . . . Oh, the hell with it!

BEULAH You're not going to solve any problem by swearing. The fact is that if you'd been a little more generous in your contributions to the party funds, you might have got Dublin, or Amsterdam, or Paris . . . (*Enraptured at the idea*) Paris!

MOULSWORTH Beulah, first of all, Paris would have been prohibitive. Secondly, the administrative capital of the Netherlands is The Hague and not Amsterdam. And finally, your allusion to party funds is in thoroughly bad taste, and ill informed. To be Ambassador in this, the only noncommitted country in Europe, is a challenge and an honor. We're in the front line here, Beulah, and the eyes of Washington are upon us.

BEULAH Well, d'you think it's quite fair to take your wife and daughter into the front line with you? I got a letter from my sister two years late. The envelope was marked, "Country Unknown."

MOULSWORTH Kindly stick to the point.

BEULAH I am sticking to the point! Very much to the point! She's moving to Seattle.

MOULSWORTH Beulah, you stick to more points simultaneously than any person I have ever known. Must I remind you that our daughter is in love—

BEULAH Yes, I've been thinking about that.

MOULSWORTH When?

BEULAH While I was talking to you.

MOULSWORTH (*With heavy sarcasm*) And what conclusion did you reach?

BEULAH (*Rises*) Well, it may just be a juvenile infatuation. It may all be over by tomorrow.

MOULSWORTH That's right . . . it may . . . why didn't we think of that?

BEULAH And then of course it may be the real thing—love.
(*She sighs*)

MOULSWORTH I don't want that word mentioned again! Now come, my dear—let us, you and I, go to her, calmly and with a modicum of dignity. After all, we are her parents, and the scriptures declare in no uncertain terms that we command her honor and her obedience. Only one thing I want you to promise me.

BEULAH And what is that?

MOULSWORTH That you keep your mouth shut and let me do the talking!
(*Turns her toward the door as the lights dim out rapidly. JULIET has assumed an attitude of tragic resignation as she lies on her bed. The American Embassy revolves away. The Russian Embassy revolves to reveal the interior. A lounge decorated in the most opulent Soviet Victorian manner. Upstairs is IGOR's room, very maritime in character. At the moment IGOR stands stiffly at attention, in the lounge, while the SPY occupies a corner of the table, a few sheets of paper before him. The rest of the table is set for breakfast*)

SPY And?

IGOR And? More I can't remember.

SPY A confession of only eight pages? It appears as though you were still attempting to conceal something. (*Pause*) Comrade Kotkov's recent confession ran to two hundred and fourteen typewritten pages, and was written in a clear, concise, functional style. At the end, the reader had a vivid impression of the author's inner rottenness. . . . You have nothing to add? (*He sighs*) Very well, let me help you. Some comrades can do nothing for themselves. Page eight, line twenty-three. You claim that love guided your deviation. Explain yourself.

IGOR   If my thoughts are simplified even further to suit your intellect, I shall soon be reciting the alphabet.

SPY   (*Deeply suspicious*)   Which alphabet—ours or theirs?

IGOR (*Exasperated*)   Oh, my God!

SPY   What was that name you mentioned?

IGOR   When?

SPY   God, did I hear?

IGOR   Why not?

SPY   Are you a believer?

IGOR   I have a perfect right to believe if I wish.

SPY   I did not ask you whether you had a right to believe. I asked you whether you do believe.

IGOR   I don't see the difference.

SPY   All the difference in the world. In the old days it was criminal to believe. With the advent of Soviet democracy, we are now given the choice of belief, or disbelief, but naturally we are put on our honor to make the right choice. Otherwise, democracy would have no meaning.

IGOR Oh, the devil take you! (*The* SPY *immediately crosses himself*) What are you doing?

SPY (*Pleasantly, in spite of his nervousness*) Belief in the devil has never been forbidden by any regime.

  (*His Excellency* VADIM ROMANOFF *and* EVDOKIA ROMANOFF *enter*)

EVDOKIA Good morning.

ROMANOFF Good morning.

IGOR
} Good morning.
SPY

ROMANOFF What is there for breakfast?

EVDOKIA Caviar.

ROMANOFF Caviar. Is there no end to this monotony? (*Hastily, as the* SPY *turns sharply to him*) I say this with all deference to our splendid sturgeon fisheries.

SPY One moment. Another subject has priority. Your Excellency, I must denounce your son.

ROMANOFF Again?

EVDOKIA Just a minute. Women have equality. I demand to speak first.

SPY The fact that women have equality gives them no special privileges, as they have in the West. You cannot expect to enjoy both equality and the bourgeois myth of "ladies first."

EVDOKIA I am the wife of an ambassador. I have the right to speak first.

33

SPY Only outside the Embassy. Within these walls the fact that I am your chauffeur is forgotten, and I revert to being a high-ranking officer of the police.

ROMANOFF Let him speak, Evdokia. It is more prudent. Let him denounce Igor before you denounce me.

EVDOKIA How did you know I was going to denounce you?

ROMANOFF No breakfast is complete without it.

SPY And now, Your Excel—

IGOR No! Let me denounce myself!

ROMANOFF (*Warmly*) That's my son.

IGOR I am in love!

EVDOKIA (*Scandalized*) A fine time you choose, I must say, with Junior Captain Marfa Vassilevna Zlotochienko arriving today.

IGOR With who arriving?

EVDOKIA Your betrothed.

IGOR My betrothed?

EVDOKIA The heroic commander of the sloop *Dostoievsky*.

IGOR But I've never even heard of her.

ROMANOFF We intended to introduce you before the marriage.

IGOR I should hope so.

ROMANOFF Don't be ridiculous. I met your mother for the first time at our wedding. There was no time for surprise.

IGOR I refuse to marry this female!

EVDOKIA   You will do as you're told! We have noted with considerable regret that you are prone to unstable and introspective behavior, and that at times you are as self-pitying as a Fascist.

(IGOR *groans*)

ROMANOFF   Evdokia, you are going too far!

EVDOKIA   Yes, and I know where he gets it from. Talking in your sleep about imperial occasions in St. Petersburg. (*The* SPY *takes out his notebook and pencil*) St. Petersburg, if you please, not even Petrograd.

SPY   Most interesting.

ROMANOFF (*A pathetic figure*)   I don't believe you.

EVDOKIA   You even sang a snatch of the Imperial Anthem, and lay to attention in bed.

ROMANOFF (*Roused*)   And what about you? Yesterday, when I took you shopping, you lingered a full quarter of an hour outside a shop displaying French hats!

SPY   Oh—ho!

EVDOKIA (*Uncertain*)   I did it to pour my scorn on them.

ROMANOFF   Yes, but while your mouth was muttering malice, your eye was roving avariciously over those odious shreds of tinsel. Deny it if you can—you were dying to try them on!

EVDOKIA (*After a terrible pause—a hunted woman*)   Have I not suffered enough without this? I was strong when I defied the Cossacks and carried vital messages under an arcade of whips to the Red sailors of the Baltic Fleet. I was strong when I distributed potato soup to our troops through three days and three nights without sleep. I have survived revolution, war, pestilence and famine. Have I now surrendered my dignity —to a hat?

SPY (*Sly*) Well—have you?

EVDOKIA (*Emotionally*) Yes, I have. I have! I admit it! I—I confess. It is a tiny confection made up of three black feathers, with a coronet of cheeky silver lace. (*Defiant*) I love that hat! Last week they removed it from the window. I thought they had sold it. Yesterday, I passed the shop—and there it was again! My life suddenly held a new meaning for me. I kissed my husband in the street.

ROMANOFF Evdokia! (*He kisses her on the forehead with emotion*) That is how you gave yourself away.

SPY A most interesting revelation.

ROMANOFF You underestimate us, my friend. Do you think that we are the only fallible beings here? What about this, which I discovered among your personal belongings?
     (*He produces an American magazine from his pocket*)

SPY (*Trembling*) You have been through my suitcase?

ROMANOFF You go through my desk every evening. I only returned the compliment. And what do I find? Decadent American magazines! Stories of drug addiction in Cincinnati. The adventures of lascivious space men! And as if that were not sufficient—postcards of an indisputably suggestive nature, depicting the ruins of Pompeii in a most unscholarly light. Explain yourself, comrade.

SPY (*Self-importantly*) I collected this material to furnish the party with proof of Western decadence.

36

ROMANOFF   The decadence of the West is well enough known by the party not to *need* proof. Can you deny that these items constitute part of a vast and well-documented private collection?

SPY   I have sent a report—

ROMANOFF (*Ferocious*)   Confess!

SPY (*With a cry*)   Ah, that terrible word! (*He sinks slowly to his knees*) I confess . . . but you cannot know the loneliness of a spy's life . . . everyone is frightened of me . . . men never even talk to me unless they need another hand at cards . . . while women tolerate me only if they want me to overlook some indiscretion. (*He weeps*) I used to look through keyholes for the party—but now I do it for myself.

ROMANOFF (*Embarrassed*)   Come, come, not before breakfast. Here's my handkerchief.

SPY   A handkerchief! When I could flood the Volga with my tears!

ROMANOFF (*With some pride*)   There is no doubt about it. No nation can confess as magnificently or as completely as we.

SPY   Ah, the relief . . . the relief!

ROMANOFF   Now, now, you are a most distinguished secret agent. We will forget your little lapse.

SPY   No, no! Never forget it! Ah, my soul! How good it is to suffer so remorselessly.

ROMANOFF (*With some impatience*)   What kind of architecture is this? One brick is displaced, and the entire edifice collapses.

IGOR   You have more experience than we have, Father. You are older. I fall in love. The chauffeur gives in to his loneliness. Mother surrenders herself to a hat—

EVDOKIA   (*Burying her head in her hands*)   Yes, my hat! What a disgrace.

IGOR   But you, Father, you only let yourself go at night, when you dream of Leningrad.

ROMANOFF   Leningrad? St. Petersburg. That is an historical fact, and not subversion. (*Dreamily*) I remember the city in nineteen thirteen. The light streaming through the windows of the Winter Palace into the snow.

IGOR   (*Romantic*)   You were outside, in the cold with the peasants.

ROMANOFF   I was inside, in the warmth with the court—planning the revolution. I was the party's inside man. My duties were to dance with the wives of army commanders and surreptitiously find out the disposition of their husbands' units. It was delicious . . .

IGOR   Then surely, Father, with your experience, you can understand me when I tell you that I am in love—desperately, whole-heartedly in love.

SPY   I understand you, brother.

EVDOKIA   Who is she? Some penniless local girl?

IGOR   Does it matter?

ROMANOFF   We—your mother and I—wish you to marry well, my son, high up in the hierarchy.

38

IGOR   But that is snobbism!

EVDOKIA   Don't be ridiculous. Snobbism was abolished in nineteen seventeen.

IGOR   I am in love with the daughter of an ambassador!

EVDOKIA (*Rises, enraptured*)   Ambassador?

ROMANOFF (*Pleased*)   Which ambassador?

IGOR   The Ambassador of the United States of America.
       (*A terrible pause*)

ROMANOFF (*His voice breaking with emotion*)   Are you aware of the words you have just uttered?

IGOR (*Standing stiffly at attention*)   Yes, Father. Otherwise I could not have uttered them.

ROMANOFF (*Suddenly losing all control, screams*)   Swine!
       (*Pause*) Saboteur! (*Pause*) Interventionist! (*Pause*) Anarchist! (*Pause*) Trotskyist! (*Pause—with a sob*) My son!

SPY (*In ecstasy*)   This surpasses all other confessions!

ROMANOFF (*With ill-concealed pride in his son*)   You will go up to your room.

IGOR   Yes, Father.

ROMANOFF   Why do you smile?

IGOR   I will not be alone.
       (*He goes*)

ROMANOFF (*To* SPY)   You!

SPY   Me?

ROMANOFF   Breakfast is set for three. You will join us.

EVDOKIA   A spy at the dining table?

ROMANOFF   Evdokia, we have lost our son.
(IGOR *enters upstairs, closes the door and throws himself on the bed*)

EVDOKIA   Oh, Vadim!

ROMANOFF (*Calm as ice*)   Caviar, you said? Let us enjoy it . . .
(*They all sit slowly, in unison, and begin to eat, struggling with their emotions. The interior of the Russian Embassy revolves off as the lights fade. As the lights come up on the square, two people enter, one a huge and cheerful American, the other a pretty but grim Russian girl. They have evidently been traveling*)

RUSSIAN GIRL   Thank you for allowing me to share your taxi.

AMERICAN   That's O.K. Anything else I can do for you?

RUSSIAN GIRL (*Cold*)   No.
(*The two soldiers enter, still dressed as vendors*)

FIRST SOLDIER   Peanuts, traditional salted marzipan, raffia table-runners. English collar studs, back numbers of *True Detective* magazine?

SECOND SOLDIER   Keepsakes, bangles, prehistoric coins, religious postcards.

} *Together*

RUSSIAN GIRL   Have you any sociological novels?

FIRST SOLDIER   Yes. *Uncle Tom's Cabin*—in English.

RUSSIAN GIRL   I didn't know it was translated!

AMERICAN You have no flowers?

SECOND SOLDIER No.

AMERICAN (*Gay*) Well, that's it. No flowers. (*He takes out a piece of money*) Give me something for that. Anything. Bangles? That's fine. Hey, do I get any change? O.K. I know the answer to that one. Americans. No change.

RUSSIAN GIRL You are not thrifty.

AMERICAN I'm in love.

RUSSIAN GIRL All the more reason for thrift.

AMERICAN See you, beautiful!

RUSSIAN GIRL Good-bye, sir.
  (*They go to their respective embassies, and enter. The* GENERAL *has watched their last exchange from an archway, and he now comes swiftly forward*)

GENERAL Who are they?

FIRST SOLDIER Search me.

SECOND SOLDIER The plot thickens.
  (*The figure of Death the Reaper wobbles out accompanied by the grind of machinery and the striking of the bell*)

FIRST SOLDIER It's Death!

GENERAL Death again? (*He pulls out his watch and looks at it. The soldiers look at their wrist watches*) Death at a quarter to nine?

FIRST SOLDIER . . . Eight thirty-three.

41

SECOND SOLDIER . . . Nine fourteen.

GENERAL It's the first time I've ever known Death to make a mistake.

JULIET (*Off*) Romanoff.

IGOR (*Off*) Juliet.

GENERAL Sh! What's that?

FIRST SOLDIER I can't hear—

GENERAL Listen.

JULIET Romanoff.

IGOR Juliet.

JULIET Romanoff.

IGOR Juliet.

SECOND SOLDIER It sounds like . . . Romanoff . . .

FIRST SOLDIER And . . . Juliet?

GENERAL Where's it coming from?

FIRST SOLDIER

SECOND SOLDIER } (*Each pointing to a balcony*) Up here.

GENERAL (*Happy*) Balconies? . . . Then there's hope . . .

JULIET Romanoff.

IGOR Juliet.

JULIET Romanoff.

IGOR Juliet.

(*The soldiers and the* GENERAL *look from one balcony to the other as though watching a tennis match. Their initial elation dissolves into a bleak despondency as the yearning in the voices begins to underline the sadness of the situation*)

Curtain

ACT TWO

ACT TWO

Noon to Afternoon.

It is later in the day. The light is no longer the pale silver of early morning, but has a deep orange glow which makes the sky intensely blue and the walls the color of peaches.

The lower sections of both houses are empty, but the young lovers are still incarcerated in their respective rooms. They are both in positions of romantic dejection.

The two soldiers lie lazily in the street. It is siesta time. One is asleep, the other is strumming languidly on a guitar. Their trays of merchandise are close by them.

JULIET *is the first to come slowly to life.*

JULIET   Oh, why must the mind hover, a blind bee, over dead flowers? And yet, maybe I like my flowers dead . . . maybe I'm not the happy, open-minded daughter parents dream about . . . not the normal, healthy modern girl who makes a sane selection of a mate after mature consideration—in a night club. . . . Do I betray my age group by thinking? Am I old-fashioned . . . and just meant for tragedy? (*With profound self-pity, and a sudden interest*) . . . Oh, perhaps. Tragedy. (*She looks at a photo of* FREDDIE) To look at a man . . . to visualize children with his eyes—and my nose. . . . Oh, Freddie, if only I hated you . . . but no, I like you . . . quite . . . in your silly, keen, determined way. . . . I never quite know what you're being determined about, but that

47

look makes older men call you promising. Freddie, you're a skyscraper of a guy. You'll hold our babies in all the right positions. . . . You'll teach them to play baseball before they can walk, and to count before they can read. . . . Only Freddie . . . I won't be those babies' mother . . . why? Because I like you, dear . . . and because I don't love you. (*She discards the photo, and takes up an empty frame*) Igor, I love you . . . but I don't really like you much . . . maybe the two don't go together . . . when I was small, I always swore I'd marry a man with blue eyes . . . your eyes are brown . . . brown like—like damp patches on the wall . . . and yet, when I look into them, I lose my way . . . I forget my discretion, my education—my table manners . . . (*Holds the empty frame close to her face and shuts her eyes*) Oh. Igor, the way the warmth creeps into those eyes against your better judgment.

(*Lost in her reverie, she cries quietly. In his room,* IGOR *stirs and leaps to his feet with romantic violence*)

IGOR   Theory is a corset. I can no longer breathe. Was Karl Marx ever in love? Are there frontiers which even the greatest of teachers have never crossed? Would the barricades have attracted so many martyrs if love had been as easy to find as death? I wonder. . . . For the first time in my life, I feel a coward. I love the sea, but I love a woman more. A woman? If I could take her home—if it were possible—they would criticize her frivolous and untheoretical mind. How I hate it myself at times. They would even criticize her looks—that vapidly romantic expression—those great gray eyes which ask endless questions, and which make me smile as I think of them—that concern with dress, with personal appearance—so unfeminine . . . and yet . . . as one who has been nurtured on the truth, the accurate, didactic truth, I must shout for the good of my Slavonic soul, I am in love! If I have to die for it, if I have to kiss the soil with frozen lips, I shall have known this exultation. . . . And Juliet, the silences! . . . Stretching so intimately into infinity, silences which seem to wander among the stars and among stray thoughts. Oh, Juliet . . . the tender gravity of our silences! (*He turns his head away violently*) Oh, how undignified to feel the hot tears rolling down where rain and sleet have hammered so ineffectually! Remember, in your lucid moments, Igor Vadimovitch Romanoff, that you are second-in-command of a warship. . . . (*He stands stiffly at attention—his back to the audience—then bows his head and says brokenly*) There are no lucid moments left . . . you are a man in love. . . . (*He sits heavily*)

JULIET (*With sudden anger*) Oh, drink your vodka with your buddies. What do you care if I'm on the verge of suicide? You probably chalk up the number of your conquests on the hull of your icebreaker! I can see you now, joking with your awful poppa about how you insinuated your way into a reactionary's heart. I hate you! (*She puts the frame down, and picks up* FREDDIE's *photo*) Poor Freddie . . . I said such heartless things about you. . . . (*She studies the picture with compassion and tenderness*) Oh, Freddie, you're dreadful . . . (*She drops the photo again*) Forgive me . . . Igor, Freddie . . . both of you . . . I'm not myself . . . (*She relapses*)

IGOR (*Rising angrily*) And yet I doubt whether you have the capacity to suffer as I can suffer . . . you come from a new and superficial race . . . we have suffered from time immemorial, and when necessary, we fall into the bitter practice gracefully and unnoticeably. . . . No doubt you are seeking

49

consolation with your father, who is successfully cheering you up by recounting his exploits on the Stock Exchange . . . it is your education I must blame, not you. . . . I know my duty . . . I will suffer for us both. . . .

(*He sits and suffers*)

JULIET (*A murmur*)   Oh, Igor . . . Igor . . . Igor.

IGOR (*A murmur*)   Juliet . . . Juliet . . . Juliet.

(*The lights fade as the interiors of both embassies revolve off. The lights come up on the square. The* GENERAL *enters in his shirt sleeves, perspiring freely. He dabs his forehead with a handkerchief. The soldiers rise lazily*)

GENERAL (*Looking at* JULIET's *balcony*)   What's new?

FIRST SOLDIER   It's the hottest day since sixteen forty-one.

GENERAL   Oh!?

FIRST SOLDIER   A hundred forty in the shade and ninety-five in the sun.

GENERAL   That's impossible.

FIRST SOLDIER   That's what it says at the Observatory.

GENERAL   Oh, does it? It must be right, in that case. I need some cuff links . . . I've lost mine at cards.

SECOND SOLDIER   Real imitation sapphire?

GENERAL   A little ostentatious—(*He points to a pair of cuff links*) I'll take these.

SECOND SOLDIER   There's no guarantee with those.

GENERAL   I'll take them all the same.

(*The* SECOND SOLDIER *hands the cuff links to the* GENERAL, *who puts them in his pocket*)

SECOND SOLDIER That's four hundred, General.

GENERAL Put them on my account.

SECOND SOLDIER But when will you pay me?

GENERAL You may be a corporal soon. Well done!

FIRST SOLDIER (*Indicating the balconies*) General, what are we going to do about them?

GENERAL Oh, don't ask me. I don't know yet. There's so little time for thought in this silly world of diplomacy. Last night during the celebration I was talking to the American Ambassador. He wanted to talk about something, but I succeeded in talking about nothing. Unfortunately, the British Ambassador saw us. I've got to see him in a minute in order to inform him that we were talking about nothing. He won't believe me. Within five minutes the West German Ambassador will have heard that I have seen the British Ambassador, and he'll ask me what I've been talking about. I'll tell him . . . nothing. He won't believe me. Within the hour I will have slid all the way down the diplomatic list and will be trying to convince the Consul General of the Yemen . . . that there are no secrets I share with the Consul General of Viet Minh . . . and he won't believe me either. And then it begins all over again tomorrow. (*He looks up at both balconies*) Sometimes I wish I could just fall in love. Then, at least, you know who your opponent is!
(*He begins to go*)

SECOND SOLDIER Where are you going, General?

GENERAL I'm going to dress again. In this sad life you always have to dress up to do the things that you enjoy least . . . and vice versa.

(The GENERAL *laughs until he suddenly realizes the implications of his remark, and he goes off, chiding himself for his faux pas. The lights fade on the square. The American Embassy revolves into position.* HOOPER, BEULAH *and* FREDDIE *are seated in the drawing room. Things have not been going well)*

FREDDIE   Well, when's the next plane back?

MOULSWORTH   You seem to take the whole ghastly situation very lightly, if you don't mind my saying so.

FREDDIE   I take it easy, sir. Hell, a girl can change her mind about a guy. I've changed my mind about a good number of girls.

BEULAH   Oh, it's all too dreadful . . . and to think that Freddie has flown—how many miles is it, Freddie?

FREDDIE   Four thousand.

BEULAH   Four thousand miles!

MOULSWORTH   That figure is beginning to annoy me, Beulah. We've had it several times already. You've even consulted an atlas.

FREDDIE   I made it four thousand, two hundred and seventeen, counting the trips to the airport. But what the hell? I like flying!

MOULSWORTH   Exactly! He likes flying, Beulah. . . . Now! I knew your father, son.

FREDDIE   I know you did, sir. And he knew you.

MOULSWORTH   That's right, he did. And what's more, I liked him.

FREDDIE Well, I never talked about it with him, sir, but I'm pretty certain he liked you.

MOULSWORTH (*A little irritated, to say the least*) I talked to him about it. He did like me. He was a fine, upstanding man, the best Number Three ever to row for Princeton, and a credit to the Navy. Do you know what he would have done under these circumstances? He'd have gone up those stairs and he'd have shouted his way into the girl's heart!

FREDDIE I beg to differ with you, sir. Dad was a gentleman. He'd never have raised his voice against a lady.

BEULAH (*In triumph*) There!

MOULSWORTH (*To his wife*) What are you so happy about? Just stabbing me in the back all the way down the line.

FREDDIE Dad would have gone right out there and clobbered that Russian.

BEULAH How romantic!

FREDDIE Yes, ma'am, he was of the "let-the-best-man-win" school. But then, he always won. He weighed 'most three hundred pounds.

BEULAH Maybe that's the solution. Women just adore brave men. Look at the bullfighters.

MOULSWORTH What the hell have bullfighters got to do with it? D'you think I want an international situation on my hands?

FREDDIE No, and anyhow I'm not a scrapper. I'm a believer in negotiation. I studied law—for half a year.

MOULSWORTH Good Lord, man. The days of negotiation for a wife are over. Nowadays marriage like everything else is strictly business, and business is pressure. Now go up there, son, and fight for your wife.

FREDDIE (*He starts to answer* MOULSWORTH, *then decides to appeal to* BEULAH) Mrs. Moulsworth.

BEULAH Yes, dear?

MOULSWORTH Oh, for God's sake!

FREDDIE I'm deeply attached to your daughter, but I think it only fair to tell you that when I asked her to marry me she never said more in reply than that she'd think it over.

MOULSWORTH In business that's tantamount to an acceptance. She may argue the terms of the contract, but she's initialed the rough draft. Now, go up there and clinch the deal!

BEULAH Oh, Hooper, do stop seeing everything in terms of business. When he proposed to me, he slapped me on the back and said, "Beulah, how about going into partnership?" Then when Juliet was born I woke up to find him standing at the foot of the bed with some flowers. The first words I heard him utter as I came out of the haze and the agony were, "Well, first one off the production line."

MOULSWORTH I got you, didn't I? That just proves my point.

FREDDIE (*Good naturedly*) I hate to say this to you, sir, but it's my marriage, not yours.

MOULSWORTH Freddie, I'm talking to you as one American to another. Julie's a girl we both love and cherish. She's in love with a Communist. If this thing goes through, it may mean that she could be guilty of attempting to overthrow the government of the United States by force.

FREDDIE Oh, that's ridiculous.

MOULSWORTH It may sound ridiculous to you and to me, but it won't sound ridiculous before a Senate Investigating Committee.

FREDDIE Well, what d'you want me to do, sir? Talk to her? Or marry her?

MOULSWORTH Well, I . . . (*After a short pause*) Whatever you think best, son. You're right. I was kind of hasty and . . . well, I'm a little sore about what has happened . . . It all seemed so great before breakfast . . . .

FREDDIE (*With a grave, deep sigh*) Well, I guess that's . . . life.

MOULSWORTH (*With a reciprocal smile*) Never said a truer word, son. That's what it is. Life . . . the great unpredictable.

FREDDIE Just when you hit a home run, why you have to go and break your ankle.

MOULSWORTH Precisely right.

FREDDIE Well, I'll go up there. Talk to her.

MOULSWORTH (*Extending his hand, moved*) Good boy!

BEULAH (*Who has been lost in a profound reverie*) One small question, Freddie. If she changes her mind and wants to have you, what will you do?

FREDDIE Oh, I'll marry her. I believe in marriage, Mrs. Moulsworth.

BEULAH   And do you believe in love?

FREDDIE *(As though it were unimportant)*   Sure, sure.

BEULAH   Then go up there, and our blessings go with you. Oh, and, Freddie, be gentle.

MOULSWORTH   Yeah, be gentle, but don't forget to be real tough. (FREDDIE *exits*) What a gutless generation. If it wasn't for the fact that I'm a diplomat, I'd rather have shot my mouth off. His girl going to marry a Red, and he talks about negotiation!

BEULAH   He's very sensitive.

MOULSWORTH   You always say that. A little mousy guy I can understand being sensitive, but a guy his size just hasn't the right.

   (FREDDIE *can be heard knocking at the upstairs door*)

BEULAH   Sh!

   (*They both look at the ceiling.* JULIET *stirs*)

FREDDIE *(Off)*   Julie . . . it's me . . . Freddie.

JULIET   Go away, Freddie . . . I'm not in a state to see anybody.

FREDDIE   I only wanted to say good-bye, kid . . . I've come four thousand miles to say it.

JULIET   D'you mean that?

FREDDIE   Sure. I understand.

JULIET   Are you alone?

FREDDIE   I swear it.

JULIET I'll let you in for a moment, Freddie, if you promise not to look at me.

FREDDIE That's a tough assignment but . . . I promise. (JULIET *unlocks the door.* FREDDIE *enters*) Julie!

JULIET (*Her back to him*) You promised!

FREDDIE Sure. Well, I guess I—Well, there's really not much to say.

JULIET How's business?

FREDDIE How the hell do I know? Dad bought up all his competitors before he died. There's nothing left for me to do.

JULIET You mean you've gone sour on refrigerators?

FREDDIE I guess I'm just . . . mature. (*He sees his photograph on the bed, picks it up*) Hey, where'd you get this awful photograph?

JULIET I don't know . . . I had it.

FREDDIE No wonder you fell out of love.

JULIET (*Pained and weary*) Is Dad very upset?

FREDDIE Yeah . . . I guess he is. . . . (*Without much enthusiasm*) He's a great guy.

JULIET (*Dully*) The greatest. . . . What can I do?

FREDDIE (*He smiles*) I know what I'd do, but then I'm not you, and I don't think any advice of mine would be much value to you.

JULIET (*To him for the first time, with a kind of interest*) Freddie, you've changed.

FREDDIE (*With charm*) Have I? (*Not looking at her*) Hey, Julie, what's it like being in love? Really in love?

JULIET Hell.

FREDDIE Is that so? Gee, I'm sorry.

JULIET What are you going to do now?

FREDDIE Oh, I don't know. Marry. Settle down.

JULIET Anyone in mind?

FREDDIE (*Smiling*) Never less than six. Put it down to my business training.

JULIET (*Turns around*) I envy all six.
(*She puts her head on his shoulder, her arm through his*)

FREDDIE That's sweet of you.
(*Pause. During this pause—*)

BEULAH They're talking. I can hear their voices.

MOULSWORTH That's not talk, that's mumbling. He'll never get to first base that way.

FREDDIE (*Uncomfortable*) D'you want me to go?

JULIET Not particularly.

FREDDIE I think maybe I ought to anyway.

JULIET Aren't you going to tell me I'm crazy and unpatriotic to fall for a Commie?

FREDDIE No, I'm not going to tell you that. You're the only person can convince yourself of that.

JULIET God knows I've tried, Freddie.

FREDDIE   Yeah, I think you have.

JULIET   These barriers ought not to exist.

FREDDIE   Sure, there ought to be no more wars, no race discrim-
ination, no bombs—everyone in his right mind thinks that,
and yet somehow when we all get together we find all those
things are still there, and just a bit worse than before.

JULIET (*With a trace of humor*)   You're not very helpful.

FREDDIE   I know it.

JULIET   I don't know what's happened to you, Freddie. You've
started to think.

FREDDIE   Sure . . . it was tough, but I made it.

JULIET   And you're a bit of a pessimist.

FREDDIE (*With a vast smile*)   What! Me, a pessimist? Not
while there's baseball. Doesn't matter where I am, Paris,
France, or this place, I have the scores phoned to me every
day.

JULIET (*Affectionately*)   There's my boy.

FREDDIE   Yeah. One thing about baseball. It never lets you
down.

JULIET   I'm sorry, dear.

FREDDIE (*Lightly*)   That's O.K.

JULIET (*After a pause*)   D'you want to kiss me?

FREDDIE   No. I know when I'm licked.

JULIET (*Very upset*)   Freddie!

59

FREDDIE Aw, it wouldn't have worked, kid. You feel too strongly for me, know what I mean? I could never get as upset as you do, and that'd only upset me. Oh, I don't talk good, but there'd be days with my great corny smile and the way I talk, it'd only irritate you. What I really need is a girl who doesn't want much out of life but what she sees . . . a girl who likes luxury but doesn't show it all the time . . . you see, I've got my problems, too. Money's a hell of a thing to inherit. (*He starts to go*) See you, Julie. Oh! I bought you some bangles off a guy in the street. I don't suppose you want them though.

JULIET No, I don't . . . yes, give me them . . . they'll remind me of the dearest, sweetest guy I ever went with.

FREDDIE Well, I'll see you some place sometime . . . maybe you'll bring your husband over to see us . . . the kids can play in the pool. . . .

JULIET (*Crying*) Don't, Freddie . . .

FREDDIE God bless you, baby. Keep pitching.
(*He leaves her*)

BEULAH That was the door, Hooper. Listen! They're both coming down the stairs. I can hear four feet.

MOULSWORTH (*Rises*) You'd better be right.

BEULAH (*Gentle*) Well, take that pioneering look off your face.
(MOULSWORTH *smiles, with some difficulty. His smile vanishes much more easily as* FREDDIE *re-enters alone*)

MOULSWORTH Well?

FREDDIE Well, I talked to her . . .
(*He lights a cigarette*)

MOULSWORTH We are waiting to hear what you said.

BEULAH Freddie, what did *she* say?

FREDDIE I don't think that we have a right to judge her.

MOULSWORTH (*Incredulous*) What was that?

FREDDIE You see, sir . . . Mrs. Moulsworth . . . I don't think I've ever seen anyone in love before . . .

BEULAH Then it's . . . real?

FREDDIE Oh, sure. Talking to her is about as hard as talking in church. Everything you say, why, you get a feeling you're interrupting, even when you're not. I can't explain it any better'n that.

BEULAH (*Her handkerchief to her cheek*) I know what you want to say, Freddie. I am a woman . . . and a mother (*Suddenly surprised by the silence of her husband*) Hooper?

MOULSWORTH (*Who has sat down heavily*) All the values of human conduct which I have learned to respect lie—scattered around me. I just don't recognize anybody or anything any more.

FREDDIE Once again, sir . . . I guess that's life.

MOULSWORTH (*Snarling*) It is nothing of the sort . . . it's an earthshaking disaster! (*Controlling himself*) Young man, there's no plane back to Miami until tomorrow morning. You're welcome to stay here, only kindly keep out of my sight!

BEULAH (*Conciliatory*) Hooper!

MOULSWORTH (*Violent*) What?

BEULAH (*Sinking onto the sofa*) Nothing.
(FREDDIE *suddenly emits a short laugh*)

MOULSWORTH (*Turning sharply to* FREDDIE) What's so funny?

FREDDIE That'll make eight thousand, four hundred and thirty-four miles of flying.

MOULSWORTH That's the kind of mentality that wins you quiz programs. And yet, young man, I look in vain for that inherent sense of moral uprightness . . . (*He grows more and more oratorical*) that desire to serve only for the sake of service, which was born in our hearts on a certain July morning —a July morning that began like any other morning—in July —back in—

FREDDIE Seventeen seventy-six?

MOULSWORTH (*After a withering look at* FREDDIE *for this interruption of his oratory*) —When the torch of democracy was lifted from the mud of despondency, where it had lain, a dying ember, and raised on high, a beacon to all mankind, in a valley where the shadows of despair had begun to lengthen, as the sun of freedom set.

BEULAH Who said that—Lincoln?

MOULSWORTH (*Spinning to face her, and stamping his foot*) I said that!
(*The lights fade on the American Embassy as the Russian embassy comes into view. The Russian family is in session.* MARFA *is holding forth, and appears to be in full control*)

MARFA I shall be forced to report unfavorably on the state of this Embassy when I return. Your secret service man is in tears. No man who is in the habit of clouding his vision with tears can be consistently vigilant.

SPY (*Elated*)   On the contrary, I am only just beginning to see! How can one understand our great and tortured history except through the magnifying glass of tears?

MARFA   Disgraceful! You, Comrade Ambassador, are guilty of indisputable apathy, and you, comrade, who should be a mirror in which your husband can see his errors, are but the distorting glass of the fun house. As for your son—a marriage is, of course, out of the question. It is totally unrealistic to embark on marriage with—widowhood so imminent.

ROMANOFF (*Rising*)   You cannot mean what you are saying!

MARFA   What is the fate of the sleeping sentry? You are all asleep at your posts. Can you deny that you're guilty of criminal negligence and sabotage by omission?

ROMANOFF   No! I cannot deny it. Evdokia! What has happened to us since we left Moscow?

EVDOKIA   We are traitors!

ROMANOFF   But why? Why? My son, you, me—is the rottenness in ourselves?

SPY (*With staring, happy eyes*)   I shall become a monk. I shall become a monk, and place my tremendous capacity for patience at the disposal of meditation and the illumination of manuscripts.

ROMANOFF   There you are. It is contagious. Why?

EVDOKIA   If this means Siberia or death—I shall go out and buy that hat today.

ROMANOFF   It must be this confounded country which is subversive—the climate—the atmosphere— (*To* MARFA) Why
do you look so sarcastic? You can know nothing about this
country, you have only just arrived here.

MARFA   On the contrary, I am extremely well informed about it.
Conditions are chaotic, owing to a moribund economy. The
atmosphere is one of sleepy indolence, and the climate is torrid in winter and more torrid in summer.

ROMANOFF   But . . . you have not lived through these summer
nights!

MARFA   Summer nights? Of course I have, in the Black Sea.
My eye never left the compass!

ROMANOFF   (*Exasperated*)   All your life you have seen nothing
except that which met your eye, and you have noticed nothing
except that which has been brought to your attention.

MARFA   Your insults do not affect me, comrade. I am sure that
I know more about this country than you do, in spite of your
ambassadorial pretensions. What is the annual rainfall of the
capital?

ROMANOFF   I haven't any idea, nor do I think that it affects the
political situation.

MARFA   Three milimeters.

ROMANOFF   Thank you very much.

MARFA   And how many kilometers of narrow-guage railroads
are there?

ROMANOFF   I don't know. We walk.

MARFA Six point seven, with another five which has been under construction since nineteen hundred and twelve. And how many secondary schools are there?

ROMANOFF One?

MARFA None!

ROMANOFF Near enough.

MARFA On the contrary. One hundred per cent error. I inform myself about everything, and as a consequence I am able to speak with authority. As for you, Your Excellency, you are precisely the type of old-style foreign representative which Honored Artist K. K. Bolshikov attacked so brilliantly in his five-act drama, *Kill the Swine*.

ROMANOFF A subtle title!

MARFA You speak of sublety as though it were a virtue.

ROMANOFF It is a mark of intelligence. (*He studies her*) Strange to have such a beautiful face, disfigured from inside.

MARFA Are you criticizing me?

ROMANOFF We have a perfect right to criticize each other. It is a pastime encouraged by the party. You have been criticizing me since your arrival. Now it is my turn. My criticism will take the form of a history lesson. Don't interrupt me— I am sure you know many more dates than I do, but I know more about our revolution, because I was there! I remember the first glimmer of hope on a horizon which had been dead for years, no larger than a feather floating on the sea, but it was enough. I am not a religious man, but I used to go to church to hear the voices. There is no people which can sing as we can, and when the liberated passion of a thousand hearts streams into the golden dome, clashing, weaving, murmuring, roaring, then a man can believe in anything, for our battle cry is ecstasy. Some nations surpass themselves out of love, others out of hatred, others by contemplating the still waters of reason. We immortalize ourselves by ecstacy—and when the people saw that flicker of hope, they sang, millions of them, and made the sky more resonant than the cathedral roof. I saw expressions in the crowd which I shall never forget, the upturned eyes of dirty Byzantine angels, the smiles of women who believe in a truth so simple it defies description. The machine guns chattered in the cold, laughing victims fell painlessly to their death, the snow was stained with blood. Other voices took up the song, other feet stepped forward, other hands grasped homemade weapons. In the morning, victory was ours, and many of the dead were smiling still. Those were the days of our enthusiasm. And what has happened since? Our land has become a huge laboratory, a place of human test tubes. Our language, so rich, so masculine, so muscular, is but a pale shadow of its possibilities. Our literature, which ravished the dark soul of a man with such pity, is now mobilized to serve an empty optimism. Our music, divorced from sadness and the twilight, has lost its anchor in an ocean of dreariness. You, my dear child, were born into this monotonous nursery, and you have never played with other toys than boredom, pride and smugness. I blame you for nothing. You know nothing. You are nothing. And worse, you are no one. Do with us what you will. I have rediscovered my enthusiasm, and I will know how to laugh even in death.

EVDOKIA (*She rises and embraces her husband. She is emotional and quiet*) Vadim!

(MARFA *goes out, furious*)

SPY (*With eyes sparkling*) Love must spread like a plague
. . . Oh, God, save those who have been immunized against
emotion . . . help those who marvel at figures of wheat
production, but who do not pause to marvel at an ear of corn.
(*Upstairs, outside the bedroom door,* MARFA *knocks*)

MARFA Lieutenant Romanoff!

IGOR (*Waking from his gloom*) Who are you?

MARFA Junior Commander Marfa Vassilevna Zlotochienko.

IGOR (*With a wan smile*) Oh, my wife. Are you blonde or
brunette, thin or immensely fat?

MARFA (*She enters*) It is my duty to inform you that owing
to the scandalous and antidemocratic attitude of your entire
family, I will be forced to denounce the staff of this Embassy
for anarchistic and fascist tendencies in surrendering to emo-
tionalism of the most dangerous and subversive variety.
(IGOR *starts laughing happily, almost hysterically.* MARFA
*is taken aback, as though slapped in the face. Downstairs,
the parents break from their embrace, the* SPY *from his
prayer*)

EVDOKIA (*Gaily*) It's him laughing . . . Igor . . .

ROMANOFF (*Delighted*) Yes . . .
(*The Russians, with the exception of the furious* MARFA,
*laugh with mounting intensity as the interior of their Em-
bassy revolves out of sight. The* GENERAL *reappears in the
square, dressed formally, with a top hat on his head, and
gloves, walking stick and portfolio in his hand. The soldiers wake up, and gaze at the Russian Embassy*)

GENERAL What a curious noise.

67

SECOND SOLDIER It's the Russians laughing.

GENERAL (*Surprised*) Yes. Has anyone entered or come out of the embassies in my absence?

FIRST SOLDIER No one. There's a seasonal slackness of business which lasts all the year round.

SECOND SOLDIER You're pretty warmly dressed for this weather, General.

GENERAL It's not without reason that diplomats dress like this. Gloves, walking stick, portfolio, three articles to leave behind, if necessary. Sometimes, in the world of diplomacy, it is very important to have a pretext to return after having said good-bye.

FIRST SOLDIER (*He indicates the American Embassy*) Are you going in there?

GENERAL I have been summoned to both embassies at the same hour, and accepted both engagements in a fit of absent-mindedness. Have you the accurate time?

SECOND SOLDIER What's the use of asking us? There hasn't been a saint in sight for the past couple of hours.
(*There is a hiss and grinding of machinery. Three saints appear very quickly, strike each other quite brutally, and eventually totter back the way they came*)

FIRST SOLDIER That's called making up for lost time.

GENERAL Men, I've had an idea. You remember this morning when Death made a mistake?

FIRST SOLDIER
⎫
SECOND SOLDIER ⎭ Yes.

GENERAL Why shouldn't Death really make a mistake? Couldn't it be that our old friend up there was just dropping us a gentle hint? And isn't it possible that our fatherland not only corrupts the living by making them oblivious of time, place, even of hatred—but that it makes even Death lazy and forgetful of his solemn duties? You don't follow. (*As though talking to children*) Human nature being what it is, legend and literature are full to overflowing with tragic lovers— there's hardly a couple who don't end up horizontal, bloody and fruitless. Tristan and Isolde, Paolo and Francesca— Romeo and Juliet— Why should that be? What is the point of suffering if you can't survive afterwards to enjoy the relief?

FIRST SOLDIER What do you suggest?

GENERAL A trick! The prerogative of the weak! Tonight we celebrate the Royal Marriage of Our Boy King Theodore the Uncanny to the Infanta of Old Castile in thirteen eleven, which led to the coalition of Saragossa, and the eventual expulsion of the Albanians from our soil.

SECOND SOLDIER Steady, sir, that's not till next Friday—and you said this morning that it was the Lithuanians who were driven out a thousand years ago tonight.

GENERAL Did I?

SECOND SOLDIER Yes.

GENERAL Well, the great virtue of history is that it is adaptable. I have a very definite reason for wishing tonight to be the celebration of a wedding, with the symbolic blessing of two papier-mâché figures by the Archbishop. So, shall we say that with the help of (*Turning to the* SECOND SOLDIER) the Spaniards we drove the others out?—the Lithuanians!

FIRST SOLDIER Doesn't sound very probable.

GENERAL The pretext hardly matters. It's the celebration which people enjoy. I mean, unfortunately even Easter has become largely a matter of eggs. Now, kindly serenade the young lady with an apt folk song . . . a melancholy one. Don't overdo it . . . not tragic . . . just melancholy.

FIRST SOLDIER
          } (*Sing softly with guitar accompaniment*)
SECOND SOLDIER

> Oh, won't someone open the door of the cage
> And set the bluebird free?
> Set it free. Set it free.
> Oh, set the bluebird free,
> It was caught in the spring, at a tender age,
> Oh, set the bluebird free,
> Set it free. Set it free. Oh, set the bluebird free.
> It languished in summer, forgot how to sing,
> Oh, set the bluebird free.
> Set it free. Set it free. Oh, set the bluebird free.
> In the autumn it lost the use of one wing,
> Oh, set the bluebird free.
> Set it free. Set it free. Oh, set the bluebird free.
> (JULIET *appears sadly and inquisitively on her balcony*)
> Before winter comes and the wild winds sting,
> Oh, set the bluebird free.
> Set it free. Set it free. Oh, set the bluebird free.
> (JULIET *smiles drably at them and throws them a kiss at the conclusion of their song*)

JULIET (*To the* GENERAL) Oh, it's you.

GENERAL Miss Moulsworth. Greetings. Listen to me. It is extremely urgent. I need your help.

JULIET You need *my* help?

GENERAL Yes. If you wish to see the Lieutenant again, you must do as I tell you.

JULIET What do you want me to do?

GENERAL Sh! Not too loud. I want you to knot the sheets of your bed, and to hang them from your balcony.

JULIET (*With some enthusiasm*) Like I did when I ran away from school?

GENERAL (*With excessive delight*) Did you? Yes! (*Conspiratorial again*) Then I want you to write a farewell letter to your parents.

JULIET What? Oh, I couldn't. As though I was going to—no. Dad's got a weak heart.

GENERAL Oh. You surprise me. Couch the letter in somewhat ambiguous terms. There's no need to hint at any rash act. Just thank them for all they've done for you and say that you have run away to join the man you love.

JULIET Even that might kill Dad.

GENERAL The fact that you're happy?

JULIET The fact that I didn't consult him first.

GENERAL Really, I am running a little short of patience for your father, Miss Moulsworth.

JULIET He's a darling, really . . . at heart.

GENERAL Must I doubt that you are really in love?

JULIET (*Hotly*) You've no right to doubt that, after what I've been through.

GENERAL Then do as I tell you, and you will spread happiness 'round you like a—like a cloak. You must trust me.

FIRST SOLDIER You must trust him!

SECOND SOLDIER Be a sport!

JULIET (*Doubtful*) Well . . .

GENERAL It is a matter of life and death . . . for several people . . . . don't let your parents go into old age with you on their conscience. It isn't fair. It isn't Christian.

JULIET Yes, that's a thought. O.K., I'll do it!

GENERAL You won't regret it.
      (JULIET *retires*)

FIRST SOLDIER What now?

GENERAL What now? Another folk song.

FIRST SOLDIER Another folk song?

GENERAL Something maritime. (*He turns away, and awaits the song. The soldiers consult with each other. It is clear that they have no idea what the word maritime means. The* GENERAL *explains with a deep sigh*) Something about a sailor . . . . (*Half under his breath*) Oh, the ignorance of these people . . .

FIRST SOLDIER
⎫
⎬ (*Singing*)
⎭
SECOND SOLDIER
  Sailor where are you?

GENERAL (*Singing*)
  Are you?

72

FIRST SOLDIER

Is the storm on the sea, is the storm in your heart?
Which of these storms keeps us apart?
Sailor where are you?

GENERAL

Are you?

FIRST SOLDIER

SECOND SOLDIER }

Are you faithless or dead?
Are the clouds in the sky, are the clouds in your head?
Sailor, my sailor, we'll never be wed.
Sailor, where are you?

GENERAL Are you?

(IGOR *appears on his balcony, a haggard figure, holding
a revolver*)

IGOR Why do you interrupt me?

GENERAL Great heavens, Lieutenant Romanoff, what is that
in your hand?

IGOR A revolver. The classic solution to misery.

GENERAL Are you aware that they are forbidden by law?

IGOR How do you commit suicide then?

GENERAL There are many other, less dangerous, methods.

IGOR (*He lifts the gun to his temple*) You are too late.

GENERAL Lieutenant, you will see Juliet tonight.

IGOR (*Lowers gun*) Really? Do you believe in the hereafter?

GENERAL I believe in the herein.

IGOR   What's that?

GENERAL   (*Who has to think what it could possibly be*)   Life as it is lived, with all its little annoyances!

IGOR   Little annoyances? You have never suffered.

GENERAL   No, and I don't intend to. (IGOR *lifts the gun*) Lieutenant, do something for me before you die.

IGOR (*Lowers gun*)   What?

GENERAL   Write a farewell letter to your parents.

IGOR   I have already done so. It covers seventeen pages. I ran out of ink.
    (*He lifts the gun*)

GENERAL   And, Lieutenant. Something else. Will you tie the sheets of your bed together, and then fix them to the balcony?

IGOR (*Lowers gun*)   As though I were running away?

GENERAL   Yes—NO! As though you were advancing to happiness!

IGOR   I am an officer, sir. I am incapable of cowardice.

GENERAL   I understand your prejudice, sir, since, believe it or not, I am an officer myself. I am incapable of almost everything, but at the moment I do happen to know what I am talking about. If you wish to see Juliet again, alive, well, happy, do as I tell you. Give me a startling demonstration of seaman's knots.

IGOR   I cannot. My mind is made up.
    (*He lifts the gun*)

GENERAL   No! No!
> (*The* SPY *sidles out of the Russian Embassy. He rushes toward the General*)

SPY (*Desperate*)   I am on your side. Help me, and I will help you.

GENERAL   What do you want?

SPY   Asylum.

GENERAL   Asylum . . . Political? . . . Granted.

SPY   There's something else.

GENERAL   What?

SPY (*Falling to his knees*)   A letter of introduction to the most austere, the most rigid and terrible monastery in your country.

GENERAL   Oh. We'll send you to the Mauve Friars. They neither stand nor sit. They walk about on their knees. Oh, a happy beginning for you.

SPY (*Grasping the* GENERAL'S *hand and kissing it rapturously*) Oh, exquisite. My eternal gratitude.
> (IGOR *is about to shoot himself*)

GENERAL (*Pointing to balcony*)   Quick!

SPY   "Last night we were as one, creatures in a dream, selflessly united in an endless waltz. From now on we are opposed, a man and a woman in love. The greatest, most exhausting struggle in the world."

IGOR (*Limp, he drops the revolver with a clatter*)   Farewell, resolution. How did you remember that?

SPY   I listened in the shadows, and took it down in shorthand. Then as I read it in my room at night, I began to feel lonely again, and jealous that such phrases should not have been addressed to me.

IGOR   Jealous? Am I capable of inspiring jealousy? Even in my present condition?

SPY   Oh, yes, brother . . . yes . . . your life is still before you, even if it only lasts ten minutes . . . while I must expiate my sins in endless penances and terrifying disciplines.

IGOR   (*With a little sigh of relief*)   What a fool I am . . . we must rely on one another to understand ourselves. What did you want? Ah, yes. Sheets. Is it for some joke?

GENERAL   Yes . . . yes . . . a joke.

IGOR   I like jokes.
      (*He goes indoors*)

SPY   Now—your part of the bargain.

GENERAL   (*Delighted*)   Boys, take this gentleman to my office and I'll be along presently.

SPY   I'd rather wait in church, if I may.

FIRST SOLDIER   (*In disgust*)   Church?

GENERAL   (*Taking off his hat*)   Well, I'll find out in which monastery the bread is hardest, the water dirtiest, and the liqueur least potent.

SPY   Thank you. Thank you.
      (*The* SPY *and the soldiers enter the church, under the clock. The* GENERAL *goes out through an arch. The interiors of both embassies revolve on. Both ambassadors*

*are at home, and both consult their watches. They are
exasperated. Upstairs,* JULIET *is writing a letter, choosing
her words carefully.* IGOR *is tying his sheets into com-
plicated knots. The* GENERAL *enters the American Embassy)*

GENERAL (*Beaming*)   Not too early, I trust?

MOULSWORTH   I make you exactly two hours late, but then I
don't know the time around here any more than anyone else
does. As it happens, it's not too important, as my Washington
call seems to be delayed. Cigar?

GENERAL   Thank you.

MOULSWORTH   Now, let's come straight to the point. When I
want to know something, I just ask. That's the way I operate.

GENERAL   I appreciate that. In my position, I have to appreciate
almost everything.

MOULSWORTH   Now—are you or are you not going to come into
the Western Community? I've got to know right now!

GENERAL   And how is your charming daughter?

MOULSWORTH   What's that? Oh, she's fine thanks. Just fine.
Now, if you're not going to play ball with us, just who are
you going to play ball with, and why?

GENERAL   Yes! She looked exquisite last night, I thought.

MOULSWORTH   Who?

GENERAL   Your daughter.

MOULSWORTH   Didn't she, though? Now lookit, no nation can
afford to remain neutral these days, not with the bomb and
economic pressures.

GENERAL Who was that attractive young man she was with?

MOULSWORTH (*Livid*) Leave him out of this.

GENERAL (*Surprised*) Her fiancé perhaps? Will we soon hear the bells?

MOULSWORTH No! (*The telephone rings*) Oh, damn it! Excuse me. (*He picks up the phone*) I thought I told you I didn't want to be interrupted . . . Who? (*Different voice*) Washington? (*He buttons his jacket and straightens his tie*) Mr. President? . . . Oh, just fine, thanks . . . sure, she's fine, too . . . Sure, and she's fine, too . . . Just fine, all of us . . . I'm doing my damndest, sir . . . I hope to have them wrapped up and in the Western Community by nightfall . . . Oh, sure. I've pointed that out . . . they've got a lot of pretty old-fashioned ideas . . . (*Hushed*) I can't talk too freely right now . . . That's it, sir, that's the situation . . . right here with me . . . Yeah, I'll do that, he'll appreciate it . . . Yeah . . . No, I don't need anything, sir . . . I'd be grateful if you could tell me the time though, sir, then I'd add six hours and fifty minutes, and know what time it is here . . . Is that right? . . . Why, thank you, sir . . . (*He adjusts his watch while talking*) O.K., sir, yes . . . Oh, and our fondest personal regards to Mrs. President . . . Thank you, sir. Goodbye. (*He hangs up*) Great guy. Hey, you know something . . . you were two hours and forty-six minutes late.

GENERAL And I thought I was ten minutes early.

MOULSWORTH Oh, before I forget it, Mr. President sends his warmest good wishes for the financial prosperity of your nation.

GENERAL Oh! Thank you. Perhaps when you next telephone him, would you express to him my warmest good wishes for the financial prosperity of his nation.

MOULSWORTH Sure. Thanks. Now . . . what were we talking about?

GENERAL Your daughter.

MOULSWORTH We were? Hey, you noticed nothing . . . nothing strange last night, did you?

GENERAL Radiantly happy, she was!

MOULSWORTH Don't tell me, don't tell me. These facts I don't retain. It's certainly a pretty exhausting life you lead us diplomats. Always celebrating, never an evening at home. (*Suddenly firm*) We were going to discuss the Western Community, weren't we, before you side-tracked me? Now let me ask you, what exactly have you said to the Russians?

GENERAL Well— (*And the* GENERAL *is saved by the bell. The church clock emits four very loud and very unpleasant chimes. He takes advantage of this, explaining the intricacies of his policy toward the Russians while* MOULSWORTH *strains to follow the argument. The* GENERAL *is discovered shouting as the chimes end*) . . . In those precise words!

MOULSWORTH Would you mind explaining that to me again?

GENERAL (*Rising*) Oh, not now, Your Excellency. You have pointed out yourself that it's very much later than we thought.
   (*He pulls out his watch and consults it*)

MOULSWORTH Yes, but I . . .

GENERAL   I have to open a bridge—half an hour ago.

MOULSWORTH   (*Very energetic*)   I must have your answer to-night.

GENERAL   (*Elegant*)   Well, perhaps we could find a moment to talk during the celebration?

MOULSWORTH   Celebration?

GENERAL   Tonight. Oh, yes, the Russians will accept, I feel sure.

MOULSWORTH   Another Independence Day?

GENERAL   (*Slightly embarrassed*)   Yes . . . Two . . . which happen to fall on the same day—would you believe it? Every three or four years you get these sudden clusters of these things. (*An awkward pause. Then, suddenly—*) Good-bye. (*He goes, leaving his portfolio and his gloves, and passes swiftly to the Russian Embassy. MOULSWORTH finds the articles, makes to follow, then throws them down, and pours himself a whiskey. The GENERAL enters the Russian Embassy*)

GENERAL   Not too early, I trust?

ROMANOFF   Only if I misunderstood the appointment, and it was for tomorrow.

GENERAL   I apologize.
        (*MARFA enters*)

ROMANOFF   What is it?

MARFA   (*Abrupt*)   Good afternoon.

GENERAL   (*Surveying her*)   Good afternoon.

MARFA   Owing to the defection of your habitual cipher clerk, *I* have intercepted the message.
 (*She hands it to* ROMANOFF)

ROMANOFF   Thank you. (MARFA *goes*) Please excuse me.
 (*He reads the message*)

GENERAL   Yes, of course.

ROMANOFF (*He reads quickly*)   Now, I am directed to inquire of you whether or not you have finally decided to adhere to the Eastern Bloc.

GENERAL   How is your charming son?

ROMANOFF   Not well. He will be leaving soon. It is imperative that we know by tonight.

GENERAL   He seemed to be throwing himself into the spirit of our national carnival.

ROMANOFF   It is a temptation which all of us must resist.

GENERAL   Oh? . . . Oh, otherwise you might become like us?

ROMANOFF   A sense of humor sabotages industrial development.

GENERAL   Really? I never knew that. How very interesting. He was with a very beautiful girl last night.

ROMANOFF   Please stick to the point. (*He consults the message*) I see that the President himself has asked for your co-operation. I quote, "At any price," unquote.

GENERAL   Really?—The President?—of the United States?— At any price?— Now where do you see that— (*He tries to pull the message toward him.* ROMANOFF *pulls the message away from the* GENERAL *with an admonishing wag of a finger*) You know more than I do.

ROMANOFF   You must know that we tap their wires.

GENERAL   Yes, I know you do, but we don't. I always find a keyhole an unsatisfactory frame.

ROMANOFF   It depends on your possibilities. Once we have taken the trouble to penetrate their codes, it is a pity not to benefit from the results.

GENERAL   Quite! Yes, it's like acquiring a degree, and then deciding not to practice—as I once said after lunch at a small function—about something totally different . . . but I thought it was rather a good—(*It is clear to the* GENERAL *that* ROMANOFF *does not savor this finer point, so he trails off, a little offended at such a manifest lack of social grace*)—well, at the time it went very well. Well—(*He rises*) I hope to see you at our little celebration tonight.

ROMANOFF   My wife is very tired . . . and so am I . . .

GENERAL   The Americans have accepted.

ROMANOFF   (*With a deep sigh*)   We will be there.
(*The* GENERAL *leaves—without his walking stick. He crosses to the American Embassy.* ROMANOFF *finds the stick, puts it down absently, and pours himself a vodka*)

GENERAL   (*Entering the American Embassy. Genial*)   I think I left my portfolio.

MOULSWORTH   And your gloves.

GENERAL   No, those are not my gloves.

MOULSWORTH   No?

GENERAL No.

MOULSWORTH Oh. Drink?

GENERAL No, thank you.

MOULSWORTH Cigar?

GENERAL Thank you. Incidentally, they know your code.

MOULSWORTH (*Beaming*) We know they know our code.

GENERAL (*Short pause*) Oh, really.

MOULSWORTH Sure. We only give them things we want them to know.

GENERAL (*After a very long pause, in which he tries to make head or tail of this intelligence*) Good-bye.

MOULSWORTH See you. And make up your mind!
(*As the* GENERAL *leaves, the U.S. Ambassador chuckles with pleasure. The* GENERAL *crosses to the Russian Embassy*)

GENERAL I think I forgot my walking stick.

ROMANOFF Here it is.

GENERAL (*Sure of his victory*) Incidentally, they know you know their code.

ROMANOFF (*Smiling*) That does not surprise me in the least. We have known for some time that they knew we knew their code. We have acted accordingly—by pretending to be duped.

GENERAL (*After another incredulous pause*) I never realized before how simple my life was.

ROMANOFF Remember. Tonight is the deadline.

GENERAL Good-bye.
> (*And he leaves the Embassy through the "fourth wall."* ROMANOFF *is surprised by this unprecedented exit. The* GENERAL *allows himself a moment of pathetic confusion, then pulls himself together heroically, and enters the American Embassy through the "fourth wall"*)

MOULSWORTH (*Surprised by this unprecedented entrance*) Oh, come right in. So, you've come to sign, huh?

GENERAL Not yet. I find on investigation that those gloves were mine after all.

MOULSWORTH I thought they were. This life seems to be getting you down. Cigar?

GENERAL Thank you. Incidentally, you know—they know you know they know you know . . .
> (*His voice trails off as he gives up*)

MOULSWORTH (*Genuinely alarmed*) What? Are you sure?

GENERAL I'm positive.

MOULSWORTH Thank you—thank you! I shan't forget this.

GENERAL (*Amazed*) You mean you didn't know?

MOULSWORTH No!

GENERAL (*His majesty restored*) Oh, my dear fellow, I'm delighted. (*He shakes* MOULSWORTH'S *hand. Salutes smartly with great enthusiasm*) Good-bye.
> (*Upstairs,* JULIET *and* IGOR *rise, with their sheets tied and their notes attached to them*)

MOULSWORTH (*Rises*)   You haven't forgotten anything?

GENERAL   No. Good-bye!
> (*The* GENERAL, *with delicious pleasure, pushes the American Embassy off, then blows on the Russian Embassy, which pivots off. In the square, he throws cigars to each of the soldiers, who catch them expertly, and places a third cigar in his own mouth.* IGOR *and* JULIET *appear on their balconies, their sheets in their hands*)

JULIET (*As she and* IGOR *see each other*)   Igor!

IGOR   Juliet!

Curtain

ACT THREE

ACT THREE

Evening to night.

It is evening, and the stage presents a scene of imminent en-chantment.

The street lamps are lit. An elaborate gilt altar has been erected under the clock. It is evidently of considerable age, and its spiral columns of tawny gold are crowned by a host of candles. There are pennants everywhere. In the distance, music, music for the open air, brass instruments and the murmur of crowds.

The two soldiers enter, in their uniforms, with guns slung across their shoulders, now more formal in appearance. They carry two life-size papier-mâché figures of the type used in religious celebrations. They have doll-like faces, staring eyes, and are evidently either of great antiquity or else made by most spontaneous and artistic peasant craftsmen. The front view of these figures, one male, one female, have a weather-beaten beauty, and are picked out in drab, subtle colors. On their backs, however, are attached priceless robes of a former age, their magnificence enhanced by their oldness.

The GENERAL *follows the soldiers on. He is dressed in a uni-form which hovers between the ludicrous and the exquisite.*

FIRST SOLDIER   Where d'you want them?

89

GENERAL   There will do. Everything in place? The sheets? Yes.
The letters? Attached to the sheets in both instances?
Splendid. There's so much to remember.

SECOND SOLDIER   The Archbishop didn't seem very pleased at
your suggestion, General.

GENERAL   A deaf archbishop can be a nuisance, but tonight he
may have his uses. Of course, he only became Archbishop
because he is entirely closed to the world of sound. It gave
him an austere detachment from reality which visibly enhanced his capacity for meditation.

FIRST SOLDIER   Look out. Here he is.

GENERAL (*Irritated*)   He mustn't come here! We don't want to
have to start shouting under the very walls of the embassies.
(*But the* ARCHBISHOP, *who is at least a hundred years old and
very small, approaches with a royal and terrible step. His
train, which is of extreme length, is being carried by our
friend the* SPY, *now dressed in mauve rags, his head practically
entirely occupied by an enormous tonsure, his eye brilliant
with ecstasy. The* GENERAL *greets the* ARCHBISHOP. *Ingratiat-
ing*) My Lord Archbishop.

ARCHBISHOP (*A querulous, but frightening voice*)   General,
this is an outrage! I have consulted many Holy books, and I
find what I had indeed suspected, that the celebration of that
most Royal Marriage between the Boy King Theodore the
Uncanny and the Infanta of Old Castile does not fall until
next Friday, and that tonight we celebrate our heroic par-
ticipation in the Children's Crusade—so kindly have those
invaluable symbols transported back to the National Museum
with all dispatch.

GENERAL (*Very loud*) Today is Friday.

ARCHBISHOP Kindly stop mumbling.

GENERAL (*Shouting*) Today is Friday.

ARCHBISHOP (*Testily*) You must speak up more.

GENERAL (*Softly, to the* FIRST SOLDIER) I surrender. I tell him today is Friday, and—

ARCHBISHOP Today Friday? Nonsense. Today is Wednesday the fourteenth. It *has* been since midnight.

GENERAL (*Recovering from the shock—very, very softly*) Can you hear me now?

ARCHBISHOP (*Irritated*) Of course I can hear you. If people wouldn't mumble so, I could hear everything.

GENERAL (*Soft*) It's all the fault of the clock of St. Ambrose.

ARCHBISHOP What's wrong with the clock of St. Ambrose?

GENERAL It has been losing time.

ARCHBISHOP Losing time?

GENERAL (*In a normal voice*) Yes, indeed.

ARCHBISHOP Mumbling again!

GENERAL (*Very soft*) Yes, indeed. It has been computed by our National Academy of Sciences that since thirteen eleven it has lost precisely two days.

ARCHBISHOP The clock was not built in thirteen eleven.

GENERAL It would have lost two days had it been built in thirteen eleven.

ARCHBISHOP Gracious. Then it's Friday today.

GENERAL Exactly.

ARCHBISHOP Then we are not celebrating our contribution to the Children's Crusade at all.

GENERAL No, we're not.

ARCHBISHOP What are we celebrating then?

GENERAL The marriage between the Boy King Theodore the Uncanny and the Infanta of Old Castile.

ARCHBISHOP (*Joining in*) Infanta of Old Castile. Quite correct. We shall then need the traditional altar of St. Boleslav and the religious figures of the young couple for the symbolic wedding.

GENERAL Yes. Now, if I may refresh your memory, Your Altitude.
(*The* GENERAL *redirects the* ARCHBISHOP's *attention to the altar and the two figures*)

ARCHBISHOP My, my, how thoughtful of you. Verily, we have an efficient President at last.

GENERAL (*Smiling modestly*) I see, my Lord Archbishop, that you are well satisfied with the new convert I sent you.

ARCHBISHOP To whom are you referring?

GENERAL The Mauve Friar at your heels.
(*The* ARCHBISHOP *smiles paternally and extends his hand. The* SPY *comes forward on his knees and is patted on his bald head, which he finds an elevating experience*)

ARCHBISHOP   He was admitted into the Holy Unorthodox Church an hour ago, and already shows a remarkable aptitude for clerical life. He has an astonishing memory for unnecessary detail, which is of great help to me. Maybe when I am gone—

SPY (*Kisses hem of* ARCHBISHOP'S *robe*)   No, no, no . . .

ARCHBISHOP   He has been absolved for one day from his vow of silence, as he will assist me with the ritual. Owing to my extreme age, my memory has failed me . . . thank God . . . before my heart or mind. I will prepare for the solemnities.
    (*The* GENERAL *salutes as the* ARCHBISHOP *leaves with the overburdened* SPY, *and then marches off with the soldiers. The interiors of both embassies revolve into view. Both upstairs rooms and the lounge of the Soviet Embassy are empty. In the drawing room of the American Embassy,* HOOPER MOULSWORTH *is having some difficulty with his white tie.* BEULAH *is trying to help him*)

BEULAH   I can't help you with your tie, Hooper, if you won't stand still.

MOULSWORTH   I'm nervous. I've taken twelve pills and I'm still nervous. How do you like that?

BEULAH   I wish we didn't have to go.

MOULSWORTH   For the thousandth time, Beulah, we just have to go. A doctor is always on call. So's a diplomat. That pact has just got to be signed tonight.

BEULAH   I never realized this country was so important.

MOULSWORTH   A casting vote is the important vote in any board meeting. Where's Freddie?

BEULAH   He went out a lot earlier.

MOULSWORTH   What for?

BEULAH (*Blankly*)   Have some fun, he said.

MOULSWORTH   Fun. I'm glad he's not marrying Julie. Positively glad. Have you finished?

BEULAH   Stand still.

MOULSWORTH   Has Julie eaten?

BEULAH   I put a tray by her door, but she just didn't answer.

MOULSWORTH   Ow! Take it easy!
   (ROMANOFF *enters the lounge of the Russian Embassy, carrying a large hatbox, which he puts on a chair*)

ROMANOFF   Evdokia, I asked you to help me with my tie.
   (EVDOKIA *enters*)

EVDOKIA   Come here, into the light.

ROMANOFF   Where is that odious Comrade Zlotochienko? Every room I go into I expect to find her there, tapping wires or thumbing through my papers.

EVDOKIA   She went out to do a social survey of living conditions here. She wants to lecture her crew when she gets home.

ROMANOFF   I don't envy them. And Igor? Has he eaten?

EVDOKIA   The loaf of bread I left by his door has not been touched. I knocked, but he was sulking.
   (*She gives a hard tug on his tie*)

ROMANOFF   Ow!

EVDOKIA   I'm sorry. I'm tired. I wish we didn't have to go.

ROMANOFF   It's my last maneuvre for Moscow. I might as well do it properly. Why do you look so sad?

EVDOKIA   I shall never be a grandmother.

BEULAH   There.

MOULSWORTH   Yeah. Feels good. Well. Time for a drink?

BEULAH   Hooper, you'd better not. Not after all those pills. Not if you have to sign a treaty.

MOULSWORTH   Just one won't hurt . . . might help to settle those pills.

EVDOKIA   Finished.

ROMANOFF   Thank you. Now, shut your eyes.

EVDOKIA   What?

ROMANOFF   Shut your eyes and don't turn around.

EVDOKIA   (*Resigned*)   Are you going to shoot me?

ROMANOFF   We'll think of that tomorrow. (*He produces her beloved hat from the box, but he has trouble understanding how it should sit on her head. He twists it to a couple of positions, tries it on his own head, then puts it gently on her head*)   You may open your eyes.

EVDOKIA   (*She does. Her hands go up to her head and she feels the hat; with a shriek of joy*)   Vadim! The hat.
   (*They embrace*)

MOULSWORTH   I've been thinking, Beulah.

BEULAH   Yes, Hooper?

MOULSWORTH How about a real good holiday soon? Just the two of us, like it was our honeymoon.

BEULAH Hooper, d'you mean that?

MOULSWORTH Never meant anything more sincerely in my life.
(*They embrace*)

ROMANOFF There. Let us go.

EVDOKIA One more kiss!
(*They embrace. The interiors of the embassies revolve away. The* GENERAL *walks into the square, followed by the two soldiers*)

GENERAL When the ambassadors appear, present arms. A lovely clean, crisp movement. (*The doors of the embassies open simultaneously, and both ambassadors appear, preceded by their wives. The* GENERAL *sees* EVDOKIA, *and tries to get the soldiers to present arms. He fails, and so salutes. His attention is drawn to* MOULSWORTH *by the shutting of the American Embassy door. He tries to salute with both hands at once, but gives up quickly*) Ah, how nice to see you here, together. (*The ambassadors greet each other coldly*) The formal part of the celebrations is about to begin. Then afterwards we abandon ourselves to more profane pleasures.

FIRST SOLDIER (*Interrupting the* GENERAL *halfway through his sentence. Very military*) Regiment. Present—arms!
(*The* GENERAL *gives a tiny salute. The soldiers are evidently very pleased with themselves. The* GENERAL *is almost in tears, and registers his disappointment in them. They still believe that they have done very well, and look defiant and unrepentant*)

GENERAL Now, maybe a short historical resumé of the character of this Thanksgiving will not be entirely out of place. Throughout our long history, we have acted as a magnet to the invader. The English have been here on several occasions on the pretext that we were unfit to govern ourselves. They were invariably followed by the French on the pretext that we were unfit to be governed by the English. The Dutch made us Protestants for a while, the Turks made us Mohommedans, the Italians made us—sing—quite beautifully . . . and these many centuries in close proximity with homesick and miserable soldiery has brought quick maturity to our men, and babies of all colors to our ladies . . . The year thirteen eleven was not a particularly eventful one in our history . . . apart from the fact that the Albanians and the Lithuanians were both casting envious eyes on our territory at the same time . . . which made our traditional policy of balance of feebleness impractical. There was, in fact, an unwritten treaty between these two powers to split our land between them. The treaty was unwritten because at that period in history neither the Albanians nor the Lithuanians— uh—could write. The situation was further aggravated by the assassination of our Emperor, Thomas the Impossible, by an Albanian desperado—disguised as a bunch of flowers. However, our Boy King came to our rescue and contracted a rapid Spanish marriage which brought Spanish troops to our assistance on condition we became Catholic. We did for a while, until the Albanians and Lithuanians had decimated each other, when we reverted yet again to the Holy Unorthodox Religion of our forefathers. It is this subtle trick which we celebrate here tonight with much pomp and majesty. These are the symbolic effigies—this of Theodore, thirteen ten to thirteen eleven, Boy King. And this of Inez, the Infanta of Old Castile.

BEULAH   I just adore history. It's so old.

MOULSWORTH   I wish there was some place to sit down.

SECOND SOLDIER   Psst. The Archbishop!

GENERAL   Ah! Silence please. The gentlemen will remove their hats.

> (*The* ARCHBISHOP *enters, now holding a gigantic crosier, which he handles expertly but dangerously, like some superannuated gondolier. The* SPY *follows on his knees*)

EVDOKIA (*Seeing the* SPY)   By all that's holy! Do you see what I see, Vadim?

ROMANOFF (*Unsurprised*)   With him you can never tell if he's not still engaged in his old profession.

MOULSWORTH   Sh!

ARCHBISHOP   We are gathered here in the shadow of our relentless timekeeper, to observe the matrimony which saved our land on one of, alas, numerous occasions, from the savage heel of the invader. People of our country! Great powers to the east (*Spins crosier to the east*) and to the west (*Spins crosier to the west*) gird up their loins for war. The regiments abound with Goliaths. We have only one David with which to oppose them—the Boy King Theodore the Twenty-fourth. He, in spite of his extreme youth, sends messengers from his cradle begging the hand of Inez, the Infanta of . . .

> (*He dries up*)

SPY (*Softly*)   Old Castile.

ARCHBISHOP   Old Castile. Although as yet unweaned, she accepts, and becomes our queen, Inez the Precocious. The marriage which saved our fatherland is celebrated again. The gifts are displayed in our imaginations. The velvet pacifier embossed with the arms of Spain, the ermine swaddling clothes, the imperial bib and tucker of silver and of gold. Hear ye! Hear ye! (*He dries up again and whispers to the* SPY) What now?

SPY (*Consulting*)   Come forth . . .

ARCHBISHOP   Oh, yes. Come forth, Theodore Alaric Demetrius Pompey, by the Will of the People, Most Divine Protector of the Unwilling. Mentor of the Undecided, Emperor Absolute and Undisputed. Come forth, Inez Dolores Chiquita Amparo Conchita Concepción Maria, Infanta Extraordinary of Old Castile, Hereditary Inheritor of Splendor, Purveyor of Wisdom, Holder of the Keys of Pamplona.

   (*During this, the soldiers carry the two figures in a slow and pompous march to positions before the* ARCHBISHOP)

BEULAH (*With a shriek*)   Hooper! Julie's window! It's open.

MOULSWORTH   She's gone!

EVDOKIA   Vadim, the balcony!

ROMANOFF   He has escaped!

EVDOKIA   He's left a message!

BEULAH   She's left a message!

GENERAL   A little quiet, please. This is the most solemn part of the ceremony!

MOULSWORTH (*Furious*)   You must have known about this—why didn't you tell us?

GENERAL (*Pointedly*) We never interfere with the internal administration of other nations.

ROMANOFF You mean you left these sheets dangling from our balconies for everyone to see?

GENERAL Very few people pass by here. Now, silence, please!

ARCHBISHOP The marriage will now be solemnized.

BEULAH (*Who has read the message—howling*) Julie! She's gone. Hooper! Gone to find her happiness with . . . with *him*.

MOULSWORTH (*Furious, to* ROMANOFF) You had a hand in this. (*To the* GENERAL) I'll get you for this. I'll declare war. My only daughter.

EVDOKIA (*A scream*) Vadim . . . he speaks of suicide . . . he wishes to die.

ROMANOFF (*Frantic, to* MOULSWORTH) It's all the fault of your confounded daughter. My son, my son.
(*He falls to his knees and weeps.* EVDOKIA *joins him at once. All through this, the* ARCHBISHOP *has been muttering the ritual*)

MOULSWORTH My daughter! What do you mean? I . . . I . . .

BEULAH (*Screeching*) Hooper. *Do* something!

MOULSWORTH Stop that man from talking first!

GENERAL (*Shouting, so that the* ARCHBISHOP *can't hear*) The Archbishop is stone deaf.

ARCHBISHOP Do you, Theodore Alaric—

MOULSWORTH   I'll get my car—

ARCHBISHOP   Demetrius Pompey—

MOULSWORTH   Search every—have the frontier sealed.

GENERAL *(Indulgent)*   Quiet, please!

ARCHBISHOP   By the Will of the People—

MOULSWORTH   Let me see that note.

BEULAH *(Desperate)*   It has no forwarding address.

ARCHBISHOP   Most Divine Protector of the Unwilling—

MOULSWORTH   I'll call Washington.

ARCHBISHOP   Mentor of the Undecided.

MOULSWORTH *(To the* GENERAL—*fuming)*   Call out your police!

ARCHBISHOP   Emperor Absolute and Undisputed . . . *(He dries up)* Yes?

SPY   Alias Igor Vadimovitch Romanoff.

ARCHBISHOP   Alias Igor Vadimovitch Romanoff.

ROMANOFF   Igor!

MOULSWORTH   Hey, those figures have grown!

ARCHBISHOP   . . . Take this woman to be your lawfully wedded wife?

MOULSWORTH   Stop the ceremony! It's a trick!
   (The soldiers block the ambassadors' passage with their rifles)

IGOR   I do.

ARCHBISHOP Do you, Inez Dolores—Chiquita Amparo—

ROMANOFF Stop! Stop! Stop!

EVDOKIA Vadim, why?

ARCHBISHOP Conchita Concepción—

MOULSWORTH (*To the* GENERAL) I'll have you bombed . . .
I'll summon the United Nations.

ARCHBISHOP Maria, Infanta of Old Castile—

BEULAH My girl, my girl.

ROMANOFF We are impotent.

ARCHBISHOP Hereditary Inheritor of Splendor.

MOULSWORTH This calls for concerted action.

ROMANOFF We have not the habit of collaboration.

ARCHBISHOP Purveyor of Wisdom.
(MOULSWORTH *makes another attempt to reach his
daughter. The* SECOND SOLDIER *aims his rifle at* MOULS-
WORTH's *head*)

MOULSWORTH (*Recoiling—to the* GENERAL) You have threatened the United States Ambassador!

ARCHBISHOP Holder of the Keys of Pamplona— (*He dries up*)
Yes?

SPY Alias Juliet Alison Murphy Vanderwelde Moulsworth.

ARCHBISHOP Alias Juliet Alison Murphy Vanderwelde Moulsworth . . . Well, I don't remember that in the ritual.

MOULSWORTH Sure you don't! I said, sure you don't!

SPY   It is here, in illuminated letters of the fourteenth century.

ARCHBISHOP   Then it must be my memory again. Do you take this man as your lawfully wedded husband?

MOULSWORTH ⎫
⎬   (*Loud*)   No!
ROMANOFF ⎭

JULIET (*Soft*)   Yes.

ARCHBISHOP   I hereby pronounce you man—and wife. Kiss your wife. (IGOR *does so*) He is surprisingly mobile. Place the ring on her finger. Now go out there, my son, and beat the Albanians! Let the bells be rung! (*The bells ring. The young married couple, who had, with the complicity of the soldiers, substituted themselves for the papier-mâché figures at the moment that their parents' attention was diverted by the discovery of the sheets, now turn toward us, radiantly happy. Fireworks crackle in the distance. The* ARCHBISHOP *emits a piercing note on perceiving that Theodore is alive. He coos like a dove on discovering that Inez too is breathing. Looking heavenward, he cries—*) A miracle! (*Then, in a casual voice, he adds—*) Oh, well, that's quite usual here.

(*Exit* ARCHBISHOP, *followed inevitably by the delighted and devoted* SPY. *The young couple kiss*)

MOULSWORTH   It's not valid under American law.

ROMANOFF   It will not be recognized in the Soviet Union.

EVDOKIA   But Vadim—to see our son so happy!

IGOR   Father. Mother. May I present—

JULIET Dad. Mom. I want you to know—
(*The ambassadors turn their back. Shyly* BEULAH *and*
EVDOKIA *look at each other*)

BEULAH Why, Mrs. Romanoff . . .

EVDOKIA (*Emotional*) Comrade Moulsworth . . . What are
we to do? Isn't it always left to the women to make peace?

BEULAH Why, yes, to see our children so happy . . .

MOULSWORTH (*Sharply*) Beulah, I refuse to let you listen to
that woman's peace feelers!

ROMANOFF Evdokia, whatever you may have said and felt,
we are Russians. You are walking into a capitalist trap.
(*A pause of indecision*)

BEULAH (*Precipitately*) Julie!

JULIET Mother!
(*They embrace*)

BEULAH May I kiss Igor and welcome him into our family?

IGOR My second mother. (*They kiss*)

EVDOKIA (*Opens her arms wide to* IGOR) Igor!

IGOR (*Throwing his arms about her and kissing her*) Mam-
asha!

EVDOKIA And now let me welcome my new daughter.

JULIET Oh, Mrs. Romanoff . . .
(*They kiss*)

MOULSWORTH Beulah, I shall not forget this. Your foolishness
has cost me my job, my dignity, and my self-respect.

BEULAH Hooper, darling, don't be so silly!

MOULSWORTH You are condoning the actions of a government which has threatened your husband with loaded rifles.

GENERAL Loaded? Yes. With blanks.

ROMANOFF What?

GENERAL Regiment! Regiment. Into the air. Fire! (*The soldiers fire into the air. Two tiny clicks*) Good!

MOULSWORTH D'you mean to tell me . . . ?

GENERAL (*Smiling*) We could only have acquired live ammunition by joining either the Western Community or the Eastern Bloc. We manufacture none ourselves.

JULIET (*Appealing*) Pop.

MOULSWORTH Baby!

IGOR (*Appealing*) Pappa.

ROMANOFF Igor!
  (*In a rush, the fathers embrace their children*)

GENERAL From now on and into the future we will celebrate this, our greatest victory in history!

ROMANOFF (*Suddenly*) Tell me . . . why am I not unhappy? By the rules of prejudice, I should be overwhelmed with bitterness.

IGOR You are not unhappy because I am happy, father . . . and because we're in a happy country . . .

ROMANOFF I need proof of that. Happy? It can't be happy without a single factory, without a collective farm, without a communal center.

FIRST SOLDIER   I thought so, too, Your Excellency—but tonight, I wonder . . .

MOULSWORTH   I don't get it, either. I ought to be right in the throes of a nervous breakdown, and yet I feel as though . . . as though I'd just had a shower in champagne. (*To the* GENERAL) Hey, what's your subsoil like?

GENERAL (*Pleasantly*)   I haven't the slightest idea.

MOULSWORTH (*Investigating the ground*)   I bet it's just lousy with oil!

GENERAL (*Violently*)   Then kindly leave it where it is! We only need to strike oil in order to be invaded tomorrow.
   (*He smoothes the soil which* MOULSWORTH *had deranged with his foot*)

MOULSWORTH (*Laughs*)   Hey, some philosophy! Here's a guy who doesn't want to own a Cadillac, on account of it's bound to be stolen.

JULIET   It makes sense to me, Pop.

MOULSWORTH (*Laughing*)   Already? You've been here too long.

BEULAH   May I compliment you on your hat, madame?

EVDOKIA (*Blushing*)   Oh, thank you!

BEULAH   It's just darling.

MOULSWORTH   Yes, that's what it is—just darling. You know something? I can't quite put my finger on it, but I don't care who signs which treaty with whom.

ROMANOFF   Nor do I. (MOULSWORTH *and* ROMANOFF *both take their treaties from their pockets, and tear them up. The* GENERAL *throws up his hands in joy*) However, I still need proof that I am legitimately happy.
   (*The* SPY *enters on his feet*)

SPY   Proof?

ROMANOFF   Have you been listening?

SPY   That is one habit I can never lose. If you want proof, hide—hide quickly.

BEULAH   Where?

MOULSWORTH   Why?

SPY   Don't ask questions, and you will see. Hide, anywhere, in the shadows.
   (*They all stand flush with the houses. Pause.* FREDDIE *and* MARFA *enter, obviously deeply in love. Gasps and whispers. A pause while they kiss*)

FREDDIE   Are there words which have not been used before?

MARFA   There are silences which have not been shared before.
   (*They embrace*)

IGOR (*Hotly*)   They're using our words.

JULIET (*Pained*)   They've stolen our dialogue!

GENERAL (*Gently*)   It is our country which is talking through their hearts, as before it talked through yours.

JULIET   You mean we invented nothing of our own?

GENERAL You invented everything—even the country, which is yours.

MARFA Why do you look at me so critically?

FREDDIE Me? I never criticize anything. I have no opinions.

MARFA (*Coquettish*) No opinions at all . . . then how do you know that you love me?

ROMANOFF A logical question.

FREDDIE I don't know, but I do.

MOULSWORTH That's a pretty good blocking reply.

FREDDIE Why do you love *me*?

BEULAH Freddie's going right in there like a bulldozer.

MARFA (*A little sigh*) I don't know, either. I have every reason not to love you. You are a capitalist. (*Amorously*) What do you manufacture?

FREDDIE Refrigerators, washing machines, vacuum cleaners.

MARFA What volume of laundry can you wash—with your largest model?

FREDDIE I don't know.

MARFA And how much dirt is needed to fill the bag of your lightest vacuum cleaner?

FREDDIE I don't know.

JULIET (*Irritated, yet affectionate*) Oh, Freddie, *try*.

MARFA You don't know . . . perhaps . . . perhaps I love you because you don't know . . . it's such a relief . . .

EVDOKIA (*Delighted*)   Ah, the disease is taking root.

FREDDIE   You're a ship's captain, aren't you?

MARFA (*With a sigh*)   Yes . . .

FREDDIE   Gee, that's great . . .

MARFA   I'm captain of a sloop.

FREDDIE   Sloop. Sloop. That's a nice word. I know what I like about you.

MARFA   What is it—(*Recklessly*)—my love?

FREDDIE   Of all the girls I've ever known, you're the only one who could possibly be captain of a ship.

MARFA   The only one?

FREDDIE   My mother, she could have been an admiral—but you, you're the only one who could have been captain of a ship.

MARFA (*Her eyes shut*)   I'm waiting.

FREDDIE   One other thing. How about you and me getting married?

MARFA   You're practical. I like that.

FREDDIE   I'm a capitalist.

MARFA   I hardly know you.

FREDDIE   That's why I ask you so soon.

MARFA   What would you do if I accept?

FREDDIE   I'd be very surprised.

MARFA   I accept.

FREDDIE I'm very surprised.
>   (*They kiss with increasing passion*)

SPY Proof enough?

JULIET I'm jealous of them already. I want it all to begin again.

IGOR With all our agony?

JULIET Oh, that was nothing . . .
>   (IGOR *and* JULIET *kiss. In silence the ambassadors and their wives follow suit*)

GENERAL (*To the audience*) It is the night. Our victory is won. Do visit our country, if you can. The fare is as cheap as walking to the street corner to post a letter; accommodation is magnificent. All you need do is shut your eyes, and in the night, with tranquil minds and softly beating hearts, you will find us here . . . the realm of sense, of gentleness, of love . . . the dream which every tortured modern man may carry—in his sleep . . . our landscape is your pillow, our heavy industry—your snores . . .
>   (*He retires into the darkness, and blows out the candles on the altar. A guitar has been playing softly through the last speech. The four love scenes continue in silence. The* GENERAL *falls asleep, leaning on the clock tower. The soldiers are sitting on the steps, asleep*)

Curtain